Good Morning, USA

A Refugee's Dream

Phu Truong

Available on Amazon.com
Author photos by John Trieu

Printed in the United States of America

ISBN-10: 0-692-87768-1
ISBN-13: 978-0-692-87768-5

Designed and Published by Two Worlds Press
San Francisco, CA
www.facebook.com/TwoWorldsPress/

TWO
WORLDS
PRESS

Dedicated to Aimee and Mia Truong

CONTENTS

ACKNOWLEDGEMENTS

I feel very lucky. Everywhere I go I have good friends around who help me. I especially want to thank the following people for their love and support.

To my co-worker, best friend, and drinking buddy, Mel Duma, you're like a real brother to me because we both grew up on the streets. When I fell into a deep hole, you were the one who put a ladder down for me to climb back up. I respect you very much for your loyalty to your wife, your three girls, and to my family as well.

Thank you to my neighbors, Tim and Helen, for your support and for treating me like a brother.

Thank you Julius Mulwa, my Hockey Haven buddy and tax friend for over 20 years.

Thanks to Mr. Michael Williams, my teacher and friend, for helping me write my story and for giving me so much support over the years.

Thanks to 'Mom' and 'Dad', Josephine and John Finley – you are like family and you supported me while I was a teenager.

To Mr. Nick Bartel, our family is so grateful to you for your kindness and support. You have helped so many refugees, and your care and generosity have given us strength.

Thank you to Deborah Robertson, the receiver at Muni, who prepares the transfers and schedules for operators every morning. She has always treated me like a little brother. Every day when we see each other we say, "Good morning! Life is good! Be happy! A good day is coming!"

Thanks to another Deborah at Muni, Deborah McGee – she's the yard starter. She signs out the buses to the operators, and always saves me a good clean bus. Almost every day we joke around together and I tell her, "Smoking will make you stay young forever, because you die young. You never get old!"

Ira Rooks worked for Muni over 30 years and was my former supervisor. He taught me a lot, including how to deal with angry passengers: "You have to ignore them and just concentrate on doing your job," he said. He taught me how to operate the bus safely and always helped put me back on schedule when I was late. He was a very fair person and I called him, "Papa."

Vicki Solls-Davis is a veteran Muni driver. Sometimes when I'm late, she takes over for me, and I feel bad because she has to work really hard without taking a break. She started with Muni the same time as my older brother, David. She's my two daughters' other "Grandma," and she never misses a birthday.

This book has taken over 15 years to complete. After the assault, when the pirate attacks came back to me in nightmares, Kathy gave me the idea of writing a book. I am very grateful to her for helping me begin. We lost touch since then but she will always be in my thoughts.

Various people have helped me complete this book: thanks to Michael Williams, Nick Bartel, and Ralph Dranow for your contributions. Thank you to Lisa Drittenbas, who completed the final editing, publishing, and artwork. Thanks also to readers Andrea Wogsland, Joan Brennan, and Edgar Phillips. I'm grateful to each one of you for helping me share my story.

Most of all, thanks to all my passengers and co-workers at Muni. I truly love my job and consider all of you my friends.

GOOD MORNING, USA

1 VIETNAM

I was born in 1966 and grew up during the civil war between North and South Vietnam. As a baby, I was very sick all the time. Between illnesses and the war, I never got a chance to go to school. That's why I never really learned to read or write well.

When I was two and a half years old, I got a fever and my eyes developed a white film over them. I couldn't see. My mom carried me around to many cities in South Vietnam looking for a good doctor because in my village of Trà-Ôn, in Vĩnh Long County, there was no doctor or hospital. Most of the doctors refused to treat me and said they couldn't help me. The film over my eyeballs was thickening, and the doctors told my mother I would remain blind.

One day my mom took me all the way to Saigon, the capital city, to look for a doctor. She went to many hospitals but all the doctors and hospitals said the same thing. My mom started crying at the bus stop on her way back to Trà-Ôn. She looked up at the sky and complained to God.

"God, what did I do wrong?" she said. "All our lives my husband and I have helped people and even saved some people's lives. Why does my son have to be blind? Oh God, do you think it's fair?"

She was crying for a while until an old lady with white hair came toward her, walking with a cane. She touched my mom's head and said, "Can I see the baby?" Mom held me up and showed her my eyes. The old lady looked at my eyes and said, "Don't worry, your baby is OK." She gave my mom a powder and said, "Mix this with rainwater and drop it into the baby's eyes." My mom took the little bag of powder.

When she stopped crying, she looked around and was shocked when she couldn't find the old lady. She had disappeared.

When Mom came back home, she told my daddy she didn't find a good doctor, but she had met an old lady who gave her some powder. She showed the powder to my dad. My dad looked at the powder and smelled it.

"Are you crazy? Do you know what this medicine is?" my dad yelled. "This powder is only used to put on wounds to help dry them out. It's only used to kill the germs. He will go blind if you put this in his eyes!" It was probably sulfa powder, used by soldiers to treat gunshot wounds during the war.

My mom's feelings were hurt, so she threw the bag into the front yard. It wasn't the rainy season, anyway. Mom walked out to the street, looked up at the sky and cried again, "God, why are you doing this to me? Are you playing with me?" Then she went back inside the house.

Ten minutes later the sky got cloudy and it started to rain. My mom grabbed a bucket and ran outside, trying to collect as much rainwater as possible. The neighbors knew my mom was already crazy with grief over my condition, but now they thought she was even crazier. To my mom, this rain was a miracle. She retrieved the bag of powder and mixed it with the rainwater.

"I'm going to do it, because he's going to be blind anyway. Why not just try?" she told my dad. My dad was scared, but he didn't object.

My mom started to drop the medicine into my eyes little by little and she continued doing that all night long. In the early morning before the sun was up, she checked my eyes, and there was a lot of white stuff coming out of my eyes. She peeled it off little by little – it looked like Jell-O.

Then she turned off the flashlight and said, "Phu, are you hungry? Here, do you want a cracker?" She held out a cracker in the dark. I grabbed the cracker right away and put it directly into my mouth. That meant I could see. My mom was so happy, she was screaming. She woke my father up and told him "This is a miracle! Remember that old lady? She was a god."

Even though I recovered, by the time I was three and a half years old, my body was still weak. Since my town had no doctor, we went to a private clinic where the man was not an official doctor but he knew about medicine. I got a shot there at least three times a week. He used the same needle over and over again to save money, so I got an infection on my butt where he gave me the shots. And then I got paralyzed in both legs. I couldn't walk.

My parents stopped taking me to the clinic, and my mom took me directly to Saigon to look again for a really good doctor. But no doctor could help me, even the specialists. Most of the doctors refused. One doctor said I needed surgery but there would be no guarantee that I would walk afterwards. I might be able to stand and walk with a cane. "Oh no!" my mom cried again. She spent two weeks and a lot of money in Saigon until she was completely broke.

She went to my father's uncle in Saigon and borrowed money to get us back to our hometown. At the Saigon bus station she was crying and complaining to Buddha again, "Oh Buddha, why do I have to have a handicapped son? My son is too young to be handicapped!"

An old man with long white hair and a long beard came over and asked my mom, "Can I see the baby?" My mom showed him the infection. The old man smiled and said, "The baby will be OK. He has a lucky face."

He told my mom three things: He said, "First, when you go home buy a young papaya – as green as possible. Put the whole papaya on the grill and leave it on until it is almost burnt, then cut it in half. Put the papaya flesh on your son's infection. Just do it over and over as many times as you can."

Then he said, "Don't worry about this baby's life. This baby will always have god's protection. He is going to grow up in a foreign country in the future. And he is going to marry a foreign lady." Maybe he was a Buddha, and he knew my destiny. Then he walked away. My mom thought he was just a fortuneteller trying to make money, or maybe he was just saying something nice to make her feel better. She looked around for him, but he had disappeared.

When my mom came back to our hometown, she told my dad she couldn't find a good doctor and she sobbed, "Phu's going to be a disabled person!" Then she told my dad about the old man and what he said about getting young papayas, grilling them and putting it on the infection. This time my father believed her. He immediately got on his bicycle and rode into the deep countryside to look for green papayas, because nobody in the village sold green papayas – they couldn't make any money selling immature fruit.

He went to one of his friends who lived in a village to ask for help. Dad didn't typically like to expect favors in return for his kindnesses, but my father had helped this friend a lot in the past. He told my dad, "Mr. Truong, you helped us a lot and we won't take your money. You are a good man." A few friends in the village volunteered to help. So my father pedaled quickly and together they helped him bring about 50 young papayas home on his bicycle.

On the same night, my mother started the charcoal burning, and barbequed the papayas. She cut them in half and laid them gently on the infection all night long. Mom asked my brother and sister to help. They put the papayas right on the infected spot. Even though the papayas were hot, I could not feel them because my butt and legs were numb and paralyzed. My mom did this all night long until six in the morning, but still there was no sign that I was better. She had used almost half of the papayas. Mom and dad were discouraged, but they never gave up.

They tried again the next night. When my mom put the hot papaya on my butt, I started to cry – I could feel the heat. They were encouraged! Then my father squeezed my butt and pressed the infected spot. Mucus came out. The infection had turned into a big abscess. My father kept squeezing and more and more mucus came out. I was screaming so loudly, I still remember it. The second morning my butt felt itchy and I could move my toes. My parents were ecstatic.

Early in the morning my father went back to the countryside. He told the papaya growers about me, how the papayas were helping and that I had gotten a lot better. They were all happy for my father and gave him 30 more papayas. My father was so optimistic, he was singing as he pedaled home on his bicycle.

My mom and dad started barbecuing papayas again that night. My leg muscles were relaxing and my mom placed the hot papayas gently and slowly for the whole night until the next morning. She kept pinching my legs until I felt the pain and cried. They did that three nights in a row; my parents and my brother and sister took turns and worked very hard. I'll never forget what they did for me. A few days later I started to stand up and learned to walk little by little. After a few months I could walk, but I was still sick and my body was very weak.

I had almost lost my eyes and my legs, and my parents had spent so much money and effort, but they still could not catch a break. I was still sick. One day I'd have a cold; another day I'd have diarrhea or the flu. For many years this never changed, and I was never able to go to school.

Finally in 1974, when I turned eight years old, I got a little bit better and I started to go to school. I started kindergarten with the five-year-olds, and they laughed at me because I was so much bigger. But I was very happy to go to school and to finally have friends. I had lots of fun in school. But the timing still wasn't right because in 1974, the war continued between North and South Vietnam. Bombs were being dropped and sometimes school was open, sometimes it was not. Many families didn't let their kids go to school, but I wanted to go so badly I begged my father. In school they trained you what to do in the classroom if a bomb was dropped. So, I learned to jump down and crouch under a table or stand straight like a tree against the wall.

Only a few months after I started school, a bomb hit the back corner of my school. I saw a classmate's arm fly over my head. The boy who lost his arm was screaming loudly and I saw a lot of blood shoot out onto the walls of the classroom. Five students were bleeding through their noses from the pressure. Most of the kids ducked under tables, but I ran outside the school. People were shouting and crying, and there were a lot of dead bodies lying around. It was very scary.

People were scrambling to help each other because we had no medical help or ambulances available. They were wrapping anything they could find around the wounds. I didn't know what to do, so I tried to help people. Then I saw a lady in her mid-40s. She was screaming the name of her baby very loudly, over and over and yelling, "Where is my baby?" but she was holding her dead baby in her arms. She cried, "Why did you take my baby away?" She was frantic. People tried to calm her; they explained that her baby was gone. But she said, "No! My baby just ate and she's only sleeping. My baby is only a month and a half old. She's sleeping."

The town was in complete chaos. After a few hours, everyone had gathered up the dead bodies. My father came looking for me, but I wasn't in the classroom, so by the time he found me outside he was very angry and nervous. He slapped me because I had made him worry. After this, the school was open on some days, but I didn't go anymore because my dad didn't want me to. It wasn't safe.

During that time, a lot of children lost their parents. Most of them lost their fathers, because the men that had worked for the previous government were arrested by the Communist

Party and sent to jail. Many children tried to escape with their mothers on boats, but pirates attacked them and other boats sank or went missing. The majority of refugees who tried to leave were hurt or killed.

Those who survived passage entered camps that were already spilling over with people. By July 1979, there were over 350,000 refugees in crowded camps in Malaysia, Singapore, Thailand, Hong Kong, and the Philippines.

Those of us still in Vietnam thought those who had escaped were the lucky ones – at least in the refugee camps they were safe from the war. Later, I would learn that life in the camps was not all that easy.

Saigon street scene with riot police, 1975

2 GRANDPARENTS

During the early 1900s, a million Chinese left China to look for a better life. They spread out all over Asia at that time. My father's parents were from Canton, China (Kwangchow, in Chinese) and immigrated to Vietnam with my grandfather's younger brother in 1920. They arrived at a village named Trà-Ôn located at the edge of a river in Vĩnh Long Province on the Mekong Delta. The river was big enough for Navy ships and lots of little wooden ferry boats to pass through and had an active harbor. Less than 10,000 people lived in this village, including about ten Chinese families who had been there since the early 1900s.

My grandparents and great uncle ran out of money, so they decided to settle in Trà-Ôn. They found a small space underneath the bridge beside the river. They couldn't afford to buy anything to make a shelter, so they used cardboard boxes. Sometimes the rain and wind made them wet and cold and miserable, but they had nowhere else to go.

They didn't speak Vietnamese, but they were lucky to get help from the local Chinese people already established there. These families told my grandpa that he could work as a porter for a little money. Not much, just enough to buy food and maybe some clothing, but it was better than nothing. My grandpa's little brother, however, didn't like this town. He thought he couldn't make enough money in this village, and he certainly wasn't going to get rich there, so he left and went to Saigon. My grandparents stayed in Trà-Ôn to try their luck.

My grandpa worked as a porter at the harbor. He carried the goods that families bought in Giang Tien and brought over by ferry, about 40 minutes away. Vietnam was so hot that people didn't normally wear shoes. But Grandpa made slippers out of corn stalks to protect his feet from the hot sun. And my grandmother found a job, too. She went from house to house collecting dirty laundry and taking it to the river to wash it. She also carried buckets of water from the river to the rich neighbors who could pay her. Her hands were raw and cracked from washing clothes in the river.

Grandma and Grandpa bought a handful of rice every day and added a lot of water to make rice soup. They shared one salted duck egg and made it last for a week because it wouldn't go bad. They ate only one or two meals per day. They both worked 20 hours a day, starting at 4am when the big ferries came in from the deep countryside. They worked until midnight and collected more paper boxes to reinforce their makeshift house under the bridge. In the winter they collected newspaper, used it to cover their bodies like thick jackets, and slept like that to keep warm.

They lived this way for about three years. By 1923, they had saved enough money to buy a small house of their own. They started a small business selling kerosene from their home and sold it cheaper than any other store in town. At first they made very little profit, but they sold large quantities, so the business started thriving. My grandpa began to sell wholesale and he also made free deliveries. People were coming from all over the countryside to buy from him. My grandpa gave them good credit so they didn't have to pay right away, and people liked that. They kept buying from him, and he kept working very hard to keep up with the demand.

In 1927, my grandparents planned to have a baby. She turned out to be a baby girl – that was my aunt. They were very happy with their small family and kept working as hard as ever. Things were going well so they started thinking about having another baby. In 1928 they had a baby boy, and that was my father. By now, the business was getting really big. My grandpa was becoming one of the richest people in town. A lot of kerosene sellers in town became jealous, because my grandfather sold it at a cheaper price and took away most of their business.

One day in autumn of 1935, all of my grandpa's hard work was destroyed. While he was out on a delivery, the store caught fire and burned fiercely. My grandmother was working at the store, but luckily she was outside helping a customer when the fire started. My aunt and my dad were at school. Only one customer was caught inside the store, and half of his body was burned before he escaped the flames.

The fire blazed over the next-door neighbors' roofs on either side of the house and burned all day and all night. All the cash they had was in the store, plus all the customers' credit records. Everything was lost. When my grandpa came back from his delivery, the store and all its contents were gone.

At that time, there were no rescue teams or fire engines – but the river was less than 200 feet from the store, so the neighbors were able to help by using buckets. All night long, the neighbors kept running down to the river and bringing back buckets of water to dump on the fire. In the middle of the night, a rain came and put out the fire. The neighbors thought that the gods had helped save the neighborhood.

My grandparents had lost everything. Their home and their business was gone, and they had no money once again. My grandpa could not pay for the damage to the neighbor's houses, and he had no record of who owed him money. No one was going to pay him back if there was no evidence of their debts. Because he couldn't pay, my grandpa was arrested for the damage to the neighbors' houses and they took him to jail. Now, my grandmother was on her own. How was she to feed herself and two children? They had no money to pay for school, so the kids had to quit school.

Grandma tried to go back to the job that she did before, but somebody else had taken over. She was in her late 40s now. She carried water again, filling buckets at the river, selling the water door-to-door. She went down to the harbor to try to find work as a porter, but no one would hire her because she was a woman. They had to move back under the bridge by the river where they first lived, homeless and poor again.

There is a rumor that my grandma tried to kill herself by jumping in the river, but some neighbors prevented her. They saved my grandma's life. One of the ladies told her, "If you want to die, go ahead and kill yourself but make sure somebody will take care of your kids. Your two kids are innocent. They can't die with you." Grandma calmed down and decided she must find a way to survive and take care of her children.

One of Grandpa's good friends owned a noodle house. He told her, "My business is not very big, so I cannot pay you cash. But I can give you a job and pay you with food for you and your kids." Grandma's job was to wash the dishes, clean the kitchen and mop the floor from 6am to 9pm every day. My grandmother had no money to buy clothes or blankets. Every day, when she went to the restaurant, she took two red bricks with her and put them in the stove box under the oven. When she finished work, she would put the hot bricks in a sandbag and take them home for the kids to hold under their covers at night to keep warm under the bridge.

In the mornings, she took the two kids with her to work. They stayed outside the store and sometimes ate food leftover by customers. After finishing work at the restaurant at almost 10pm, she would walk home and collect clothes for ironing from the neighbors along the way. When she got home, she would do the ironing by dim candlelight and a kerosene lamp. She often got sleepy and didn't dare burn the clothes, so instead the hot iron often burned her hands. The next morning on the way to the restaurant, she would leave the freshly ironed clothes at people's homes.

The man whose body got half-burnt in the fire kept asking his son about my grandpa's family. His son told him that my grandfather was in prison, my grandma was very weak from the loss and suffering from being homeless again, and my father and aunt couldn't go to school. This man felt guilty, because he was the arsonist; he been hired by another kerosene business to burn down my grandpa's store.

He didn't realize his actions would cause my grandpa's family so much pain and regretted what he had done. He had been one of those early customers who benefited from my grandpa's easy credit assistance to poor families. He told the police the truth and turned himself in. But he didn't tell them who hired him. The reason he took the job to burn my grandfather's store was because he needed money for his son, who was in the hospital at the time, and the man couldn't pay the bills

After the man confessed to the police, my grandpa was set free. The man asked my grandpa to forgive him, and soon after, he died of his injuries.

The government gave back the land where my grandparents' house had been, and after the neighbors found out what had happened, they forgave my grandpa of any debts and no longer asked for damage payments.

When Grandpa came home, he had to start his life over. He went back to the harbor and worked as a porter, but he wasn't as strong as he had been before. He couldn't afford to buy clothes or shoes. He again took cornhusks and stacked them up and sewed them together to make sandals. Then he tied a string around his foot to hold them on. He ate only one sweet potato a day. They used all the money for food for the kids. No money for food for him and his wife.

He was overworked and he got weaker and weaker. He couldn't handle this backbreaking life anymore, and he passed away at age 46. My aunt was just eight years old and my father was seven. My grandmother couldn't handle two little kids on her own, so she had to give one of the children away. She decided it would be my father. She would keep my aunt because she was big enough to help her in the noodle shop. Grandmother sent my father to her brother-in-law, Grandpa's little brother who had gone to Saigon.

While Grandpa and Grandma had been struggling in Trà-Ôn, my grandfather's younger brother had opened a small wine and whiskey business in Saigon. He had been working hard for 10 years and his business was prospering. He was now delivering whiskey to all of South Vietnam – almost half the country – and had become very successful. The name of his wine was Ngu Gia Bi, and it had become a very popular brand.

My father went to live with his uncle and his wife, and although they already had a son and a daughter, they treated my father just like one of their own children. He sent my father to school and took care of him from age seven to 19. That's why we always called him "Grandpa" instead of "Great Uncle." He was a very benevolent man, generous and helpful to others. He believed in Buddhism and he regularly donated money to the temple to buy rice for the poor.

My dad was trained in chiropractic and Chinese medicine. When he turned 19, "Grandpa" opened a Chinese herbal store in our hometown of Trà-Ôn for my dad to run and Dad moved back from Saigon. When poor people came to the herbal store and couldn't afford to buy medicine, my father always gave it away for free. Grand Uncle supported him. He said, "Remember, your job is not just to make money. Your job is to help people."

Porters who hurt their arms or shoulders from carrying heavy loads would come into the store and ask my father to help ease their aches and pains, and he always did. Because they were so poor he didn't charge them for the treatments and even gave them medicine patches for free. Because he never asked for payment, the store wasn't making any money, and the business started going under. So my great uncle would come to Trà-Ôn every six months and provide money to keep the store going.

When the herb store needed to be restocked, my grandmother would go to another city called Cần-Thơ, the second largest city in South Vietnam, to order the necessary medicines. Although my grandmother couldn't read, she would bring a list of items that my father had written out.

In the store in Cần-Thơ, my grandma saw a young lady, a teenager. She was very surprised to see that when the young lady took my father's list, she could read it – and quickly. My grandmother was surprised to see a girl that could read and write Chinese characters, because in China at that time, girls were not yet allowed to go to school. Seeing that young lady gave her an idea: *this girl would make a good wife.*

3 MOM AND DAD

My mom was born in China in 1930. She grew up in a Hakka traditional family fort called a "Tulou" in the mountains of Canton (Kwangcho or Guangzhou) province. When she was only three years old, her father left her family and went to Vietnam to look for a better life. Years passed, and they never heard from him. The family constantly worried about my grandfather and nobody knew where he was.

After about seven years, a neighbor returned from a trip to Vietnam and told my mom's family that he had run into my mom's father in Vietnam. Their whole family was so happy and excited to finally know where he was. But there was bad news: my grandfather had married someone else in Vietnam. That's why he had not contacted the family for so long.

Soon, my grandmother decided to leave her two daughters in China and go look for her husband in Vietnam. My mother was about 10 and her sister was two years younger.

When their mother left, they went to live with my grandmother's father, my great grandpa.

Every morning my mom followed her grandpa to the farm. His wife had already died, and he wanted my mother to help him on the farm and to do the housework. As they walked, he pointed out the roads so she wouldn't get lost.

"Lan," he said, "this way goes to downtown, and this way goes to the boy's school."

Every day, Grandpa carried a wooden wine bottle strapped around his shoulder. By noon, he would be drunk on Chinese rice wine. Then he would pass out and usually wake up around 2pm. So, my mom had two free hours while he was asleep. My mom used these two hours of freedom to run to the boy's school, dragging her little sister with her. It took about half an hour to run to the school and half an hour to run back, so she only had one hour at the school. She had to make sure to get back quickly so her grandpa wouldn't wake up and find her missing. If he found out that she was going to school, he would be angry.

At the school, she left her little sister in a corner where she could play. Mom crouched outside a window and peeked through where she could watch the teacher write words with chalk on a blackboard. There were only male teachers and male students at the school. My mom copied the words and wrote them on a piece of clay that she got from the rice paddy. She learned two or three words a day. Afterwards, she would break the clay pad so no one would find it.

The school only accepted boys, and only rich families could afford to send their sons to school. Girls could not get schooling, because the old-fashioned Chinese thought it was a waste of money to pay for a girl's education. When a girl grows up, she going to marry somebody and then belong to her husband's family, so why waste money on a girl's education? But my mom didn't agree. She loved learning.

In the evening, when they went home, my mom prepared dinner and then did the laundry. She worked really quickly and completed all her farm work so that after everybody went to bed, she could practice her characters by writing them with a stick in the dusty backyard by the light of a small lantern. During the full moon she would study by moonlight. When they went to town, my mom would look for an old newspaper, and she would hide it and take it home so that she could practice reading it.

My mother's mother decided to stay in Vietnam, but she kept in touch with her daughters and sometimes sent money. My mom continued learning on her own for about eight years, teaching herself to read and write Chinese. In late 1940, her grandpa passed away. After that, the family sold Grandpa's property and sent my mother and my aunt to Vietnam to be with their mother. They traveled by cargo ship, paid for by my mother's uncle. It was easy for my mom to travel and find the way to her mom's new home because she could read the signs along the way.

Her mom was living in Cần-Thơ, with her husband's younger brother, whom she had known in China. Her husband would not leave his new wife, so my mom and aunt came to live with their mom and her brother-in-law. My great uncle had the herb store, and that is where my grandmother found my mother working.

When my father's mother saw my mom working in the herb store, filling orders quickly from huge drawers with hundreds of herbs, she saw that my mom was special. Grandma went to my father and said, "You're 19, old enough to get married. I found a girl for you, and she is special, she can read and write." So my grandmother went back to the store in Cần-Thơ and proposed on behalf of my father. My mother's parents said yes.

Mom's mother told her, "We have found a family for you. He's a good boy." My mom was very shy but she agreed, even though she had never seen my dad. They had a wedding in 1948. Mom was about 18.

After they married, my father kept tending to sick people at the herb store in Trà-Ôn. My father never forgot what my grand uncle told him: "Just be a good doctor. Whatever we can do to help people, we just help them." Sometimes customers said, "Mr. Truong, I need to buy medicine but I'll pay you later when I get paid." My father knew that these families were so poor that even thought they worked hard, they earned just enough to buy food to support their families for the day. How could they have enough money to pay for medicine? So my father always helped them and said, "Don't worry, just take the medicine and pay later if you can." He told my mom that if he charged them, then they would not have any food for their kids for the whole day.

Because my father was so benevolent all his life, I believe that's why I am still alive after four near-death experiences. All of my family has prospered because of his generosity. Thanks to his good deeds, luck has followed us through the generations.

One day, my father found out that his childhood friend had a very serious illness. The man was very poor and couldn't pay. The man said, "All of my family just eats sweet potatoes. We don't have money for rice," the poor man said.

"The medicine for your illness is very expensive," my father explained. "So expensive that even I can't afford it." But he knew that without it, the man was going to die very soon. My father went to Grand Uncle at the store in Cần-Thơ and he helped my father purchase the medicine for this man.

My father cooked the medicine in a special clay pot. He told the man to come and take the medicine once a day, which he did for about six months. After six months the man felt he was getting better. He was gaining weight and had energy again. My dad said he didn't have to take the medicine anymore because he was well. The poor man brought his whole family to my dad and bowed deeply to him.

"Mr. Truong, from now on my whole family will be your slaves," the poor man said.

My dad would never allow that. He said, "No, I am happy to help you. Just be a good man and take care of your family."

The man asked my dad to accept a small ivory pendant, carved into the shape of a goddess, hanging on a thin piece of string.

"This necklace is not expensive, but it is the only thing I have. It is precious to me because it is a family heirloom," he said. "It has been in my family for three generations, and I want you to have it. It was passed down from my grandpa, and his grandfather gave it to him. He told him not to sell it no matter how hungry he might be, because it is a link to the generations."

The man bowed to my father. "Even when my wife was starving to death I didn't sell the necklace, because she wouldn't let me. She saved what food we had for the kids and that's why she died. She sacrificed herself to save the kids. If I had known she was dying, I would have sold the necklace to save my wife's life; but she died in the middle of the night." The man's wife had died 10 years earlier. If my dad had been there to help, maybe his wife would still be alive.

My father refused the necklace. The man said if he didn't accept it, he would rather be dead. "If I had died, the pendant would mean nothing. But since you saved my life, I want you to have it and pass it down to your generations."

So my father took it and promised him he would keep it for the next generation. My father gave it to my sister, who gave it to me for my daughter, and I am saving it for her.

Mom and Dad, around 1955 in Vietnam

4 BUDDHA PROTECTS

After Mom and Dad got married, they ran the herb store for a few years. In 1954, my parents had their first child, my older brother, David. They were very content, because he was a very smart baby and easy to raise. My parents could bring him to the store or put him anywhere, and he stayed quiet while they did their business or housework. That made my parents want another baby, so, in March 1957, my sister Nora was born.

My sister was very cute, but she was mean and loud. My parents were still happy, though, because business was thriving after her birth. My parents thought, "This is good, two babies are enough." They didn't plan on having another baby. So, my mom was surprised to be pregnant again with me, during the civil war in 1965. Mom miscalculated, and on August 18, 1966, she was on her way to her uncle's birthday party in Saigon, riding in a *sit lo* (a tricycle taxi) when she started having labor pains and her water broke. She told the sit lo driver to take her to the hospital, and that's where I was born.

From the beginning, I was not an easy baby. I got sick all the time. My father consulted a fortune-telling book and found out that the date and time of day I was born caused me to be incompatible with the rest of the family, especially my mom and grandma. If I had been born a girl, everything would have been OK, but according to the date and time I was born, my fortune said I would bring a lot of bad luck. "If you had been born a girl, your life would have been wonderful, but since you're a boy, you will have a lot of problems with your health," Dad said.

My father was afraid that I would bring bad luck to the family, so he put me in the care of another family until I turned seven years old. This was not an uncommon thing to do in Chinese families. My new host family lived about a half an hour's walk from my home and every day my parents came to see me. I called my newly adopted parents Mom and Dad, too. The family that raised me for those years had three daughters but no son, and they loved me like their own son. I liked it because I thought I had two daddies. And it did seem to help my health improve.

When I was seven, my father thought that everything was better. I was more grown up now, and maybe all of my problems had passed. So I came back to the family. But soon after I returned, my father's mother passed away. This scared my father – he was sure I was bringing bad luck on the family. So, he decided to send me to the Phuoc-Hau Buddhist Temple. In those days, many people brought ill family members to live in the temple and this is still commonly done. My father thought that Buddha would help protect me and give me a better life in the future.

This was 1973. I stayed in the temple for about a year and a half with more than 50 monks. The temple was not very far from our house, so I came back home once a week and stayed the night.

The head priest of the temple was a small, nice-looking man in his early 60s with a big heart. He came to the temple when he was six years old. I called him "Thay" or "Master." He always took care of me, since I was the only kid there. Early in the morning, he would wake me up and take me to the *shai* (the sanctuary hall of the Buddha). We would bow down on our knees onto the tile floor and pray to Buddha for about an hour.

The monks had a garden where they grew vegetables, rice, and fruit trees. They said, "Our food is a gift from the gods." They trained me to not waste food. My father also taught me when I was little that homeless people were looking for food in garbage cans because in a previous life they wasted a lot of food. That scared me, and ever since then I've always finished everything on my plate. I teach my children the same thing. Even all these years later I tell my daughter at a buffet, "Just take a little. You can always go back for more."

At lunchtime I sat next to Master, and after lunch he taught me everything about life. He taught me how to love people. I will never forget what he said. "It doesn't matter what kind of religion a person believes in. Any god – they are all good. We have to respect other religions. God is always with us humans, no matter what kind of person we are."

"When you grow up," he said, "if you want people to respect you, you have to respect them first." He told me, "Just be happy, stay happy and keep smiling. One smile equals ten vitamin tablets. If you keep yourself happy at all times, you will forget your doctor and always stay young."

He told me a story about a monk. In China, they made a movie about this story. A long time ago, a monk spent almost his whole life in the temple and he knew that when he died he would go to heaven and become a Buddha.

One day, while he was on his way to heaven, a robber stopped him. He told the robber, "I'm a monk, I have no money." The robber said he didn't care. He would be forced to kill in order to get food or clothing. The monk said, "Have you ever thought, if you kill somebody, who will support the person's family that you killed? The family will starve to death. Why don't you get a job instead of killing people?"

The monk talked with him for a long time and eventually the robber became filled with regret. He told the monk, "You are on your way to heaven to become a Buddha. Can you take my heart to God? Tell God that I regret what I have done and that I accept any kind of penalty. Please forgive me." Then the robber took out a knife and cut his own heart out. The monk wrapped it up and took it with him on his way to heaven.

After three days, the heart started to stink, so the monk threw it away. When he reached heaven, he bowed down to God. He was ready to become a Buddha. God asked, "Haven't you forgotten something?"

"No," the monk said.

"Don't you have a repentant person's heart to turn in to me?" God said. The monk was shocked.

"Oh, that fellow was violent and an abuser; we don't need to be concerned about him," he replied.

"If you are so selfish then you cannot become a Buddha. As gods, we have to open our hearts and forgive, no matter what. It doesn't matter how bad a person is. If a person regrets his mistakes, we forgive him." God told the monk he could not become a Buddha. Instead, the robber who punished himself and took his own heart out to give to god became a Buddha, because he knew that what he did was wrong and he asked for forgiveness.

"If you do something wrong, and you correct it, Buddha will forgive you," Master told me. "If you help somebody by doing a good deed, you will be happy the whole day. But if you do a bad thing, you'll be scared all the time because you'll be afraid something bad will come back to you." I learned from him, *"what goes around, comes around."*

After my brother, sister, and I, were born, my father's herb store was getting busier, but he wasn't making a profit. Every month Grand Uncle had to cover the business for my dad. Finally he told my dad, "It's not good for the business to keep losing money." And my mom said, "It's good to help people, but we have to help our kids first." Mom and Dad were so poor now they didn't even have enough money for new clothes. Mom told him to change the business to a grocery store. My father thought about it and agreed. He still wanted provide Chinese medicine though, because a lot of people in this small town needed his help.

After my father converted the business to a grocery store, we had another problem – people stealing. Especially on the Chinese New Year, when it was so crowded with people shopping. In Vietnam, the Chinese New Year is just like Christmas shopping season here in the States – crowded and busy. A lot of people were stealing boxes of sesame rice crackers and candy for the New Year.

My sister Nora caught a lady who was stealing from the store. The lady was about 35 years old. My sister, who was only 10 or 12 at the time, saw her put a package of crackers under her shirt. Nora grabbed the lady's shirt, slapped her and pulled her hair. She had a hot temper, and she was really mad. She grabbed the crackers and threatened to turn the woman in to the police station. My dad stopped my sister. He told the thief, "Just try hard to get a job. Don't give up," and he let her go. My sister was so angry. She asked my father, "Why did you do that?"

"Nobody was born to be a thief or a bad person," he said. "Just because of life circumstances, because they're having a hard time, that's why they become a thief. They have to steal because they are so poor. That lady has no job, no money, and she has kids. If you turn her in to the police she will go to jail, and what will happen if she has two or three kids or old parents at home waiting for food? How will she support them if she's in jail? Her relatives will starve to death, right?" my father said. "And you will be the murderer." My sister was still mad, but she thought about this and she understood.

From left to right: Mom, David, Grandma, Dad and Nora
1960, Vietnam

5 DADDY

At four in the morning, before the vendors at the floating market started selling vegetables, Daddy used to clean the Buddhist shrine at Phuoc Hau-Temple near our home in Trà-Ôn. Daddy was a muscular man in his 40s, known and respected by everyone in the town. While he swept the fallen leaves, people passed by and greeted him, "Hello, Mr. Truong!" The temple was not far from the bridge where my grandparents first built a shack and settled here in the 1920s, just a short boat ride up the Hau River.

We had two houses before the Communists came. We lived upstairs, and both buildings had businesses on the ground floor – one was a grocery store, and the other was a coffee shop. My dad took care of the grocery store, and we opened the store's metal gates every morning at 6am. My sister Nora took care of the coffee shop. That's where she met her future husband, who always came into the cafe for an afternoon coffee after soccer practice. He started helping her in the shop, and she liked him.

Our houses were made of cement, but houses on the outskirts of Trà-Ôn had roofs made of banana leaves. When it was hot, there was a nice fresh breeze that came from the river, where there was also a floating market. Vendors brought their boats from the countryside to sell jackfruit, coconuts, bananas and all kinds of tropical fruits. We slept on simple wooden beds covered with a mat and used a thin sheet to keep us warm. At night, we let our seven cats run around, and didn't feed them so that they would be hungry and keep the rats out of the house.

Even though we spoke Vietnamese at the grocery store, at home we spoke Hakka Chinese, which is one of 50 Chinese dialects. All the Chinese in Vietnam learn Mandarin when they go to school, even if they are Hakka, and we also learned Cantonese at school in Saigon.

When I was about five or six years old, I asked my Daddy, am I Chinese, or am I Vietnamese?"

"Your grandfather came from China, and your grandmother came from China," he said. "That makes you Chinese." That was the first time I understood the difference. *Oh, I am Chinese; I am not Vietnamese.*

One time, I was sitting on my daddy's lap at the grocery store, and I saw a lady stealing a package of rice crackers. I tried to jump down to stop her, but he grabbed the back of my shirt and stopped me. "Daddy, look! That lady is stealing!" I said. He calmly looked at his newspaper and ignored her. "How do you know she doesn't need it to feed her family?" he said. I imagined the lady's kids at home, waiting for her. "What would happen if she went to jail? Who would take care of her children?" he said. Daddy always turned a blind eye when poor people stole food from his store.

"If I look at a thief, she will be scared to steal, and she might run away. But if I don't look, we might save her kids from hunger," he said. The lady took her crackers and left.

I ran to tell my mom. "Mom, Daddy let a lady steal food! He let her go!"

"That's your dad," she answered. "The only way he can be happy is when he knows he is helping people. Maybe it's like his hobby. If he sees poor people and if he can't help, he can't feel happy." That's how my father was. He'd rather be poor if it would help make other people happy.

In March 1978, when I was 11 years old, my dad got very ill. He went to a doctor in Cần-Thơ, a larger city near our village. The doctor said he was diabetic and that his liver was very dry. They gave him medicine, but the medicine didn't help. Daddy just felt tired all the time and stayed in bed. He kept getting worse. He used to be a big, healthy man, but now it looked like his body was shrinking.

Finally Mom said, "He's very weak. He can't stand up. Let's take him to the hospital in Saigon." Even after the Communists changed the name to Ho Chi Minh City, to us it was still Saigon.

It was May, just before the rainy season. My mom and sister took him on a five-hour bumpy bus ride from the countryside to Saigon, stopping all the time to pick people up along the way. They took him to a Chinese hospital, Tieu Chau Hospital and I stayed in Trà-Ôn all by myself. We closed the store when my father got sick, and the neighbors fed me because they loved my father. They were good neighbors.

A few days later my sister came home. "It's your turn to visit Daddy," she said, so I took the bus to Saigon. My mother was staying by his side night and day in the hospital. They had a bed for her there. But since I was so young, I stayed at my uncle's house nearby. We called this uncle "Grandpa," because he and his wife had raised my Dad. This is also the house where my older brother David had been hiding before he escaped from Vietnam a month before. It was right after David left that Daddy starting getting so sick.

On April 30 1975, the 20-year long civil war had ended when the North Vietnam People's Army took Saigon, the capital of South Vietnam. They began putting all South Vietnamese soldiers into re-education camps. The South Vietnamese government had required all young men to go into the military, so that meant over one million soldiers were imprisoned – including my brother, David. Many were tortured and abused. There was malnutrition, illness, and a high death rate in the camps. That's why officials in the South Vietnamese government and military were the first ones to leave Vietnam, especially the higher ranking ones. Immediately after the Fall of Saigon, 100,000 soldiers and officials were evacuated with the assistance of the U.S. military.

Before David went in to the military, my dad used to play tennis and other sports with lots of people in the government and they called him "Uncle," as a sign of respect. Thanks to my father's influence, David became a military guard instead of a regular South Vietnamese soldier. He guarded the city gate around our little village of Trà-Ôn and never fought in the war. But even so, when the Communists came they put David in a reeducation camp. He managed to get out, and he did not want to go back. So he and his wife fled to Saigon where David stayed in hiding for three years.

The new Social Republic government began redistributing wealth and property. They took the money from the rich people, divided it, and gave all families $200. This was the first time they redistributed the wealth. Then, they did it again. They took our house with the coffee shop.

At that time, there were a lot of Chinese-run businesses in South Vietnam, and the communist government was especially hard on them. They taxed them, repressed their activities and confiscated their businesses. Between 1975 and 1979, about 200,000 ethnic Chinese fled Vietnam.

In 1978 alone, at least 100,000 civilians fled South Vietnam headed for refugee camps in Hong Kong, Malaysia, Thailand, and the Philippines. Most left by boat, even though there was a 90% chance they would not survive the crossing. The little wooden fishing boats now carrying hundreds of refugees were not meant for open water. Overloaded with too many people, they often hit a storm and capsized, killing everyone on board. Sometimes the passengers were arrested by the government and sent to jail. And then there were the pirates. Pirates killed, gang raped, and maimed the passengers in unspeakable ways. Still, many people risked the passage. Others walked overland to Cambodia and then on to Thailand. But walking wasn't safe either, as there were many thieves along the way who would rob or kill for your money. There were also wild animals to worry about.

After David went into hiding, the Communists kept coming around our house asking, "Where's your son?" Mom would always answer, "He's away at boarding school in Saigon." Leaving the country was now an illegal act and the Communists were always monitoring people.

David was kind of quiet and not very social, but he was always very smart, always first in his class. I didn't know him that well because he was 10 years older than me, but he always had my back. He's the only one of us three kids who finished

Chinese high school, and that was considered a lot of education.

After three years of David being in hiding, it was strange to wake up one night and hear his voice. Only a thin curtain separated our beds, and I heard him talking with my mom.

"Ma, last week I saw Uncle Eight," David said.

"They're getting ready in a month."

Uncle Eight was one of my Dad's friends. We called anybody "Uncle" when we wanted to show respect. His real name was Tan, and he was kid #8 in his family, so Mom and Dad called him "#8 Tan." Vietnamese families are always big, so a lot of people use this system: #8 followed by the name or #7 followed by the name, etc. But to be respectful, we kids couldn't call him by his name, Tan, so we just called him "Uncle Eight." He had once been very sick with a liver problem, and my dad saved his life. My dad saved many people, and everyone in our small town loved him and respected him for that.

Uncle Eight owned several fishing boats, and now he was preparing those boats to transport hundreds of people out of Vietnam.

"What do you think?" David asked my mother.

"Well, if we have a chance, take the chance and go."

"What about you and Dad?"

"Don't worry about us," she said. "We can go or not go, it doesn't matter. We are old. If you go, what country will you go to?" she asked.

"America, USA," David said. USA? David was getting ready to leave Vietnam! And he was going to America! I felt very excited. But I pretended to be asleep and didn't say anything. They couldn't let anyone to know he was leaving – it would be dangerous if people talked.

I thought about my dad's American friend, a high-ranking soldier who spoke Vietnamese. He and Dad had been friends for about 10 years and always got together to play tennis or basketball. My dad met lots of American soldiers, because he was trained in chiropractic and Chinese medicine, and they used to go to him to fix their wrist or back injuries from playing sports.

The American soldiers always had lots of food – including chips, rice, and cookies. Every time my dad and his friend got together to play, I would go along and watch. The American drove an army jeep and always brought me Coca-Cola and chocolate. Oh, I loved it! At home, we usually ate pork and vegetables. Sometimes we made steamed fish, and we always ate soup. At parties we killed a chicken. We always had lots of food, but I liked the American food better.

The next day, David and his wife went back to Saigon. Then they left Vietnam for good in April 1978, with three uncles and one cousin in one of Uncle Eight's boats. My brother and uncles went for free, because Uncle Eight wanted to repay my father for saving his life.

I didn't know it, but Dad had been planning for me to escape with David and his wife. But then he changed his mind. He only had two sons. What would happen if he lost both of them? One of his sons had to survive to continue the family name. It was too risky. Instead, he planned for me to go with my older sister, Nora.

But then, two months went by, and we hadn't heard from David and his wife. We didn't know yet if their boat had survived the journey. My dad was very worried. Daddy started getting sicker and weaker from worry and stress. Now, he was in the hospital.

In Saigon, I rode my bike to the hospital three times a day to bring food from Grandpa's house. I pedaled barefoot and wore a raincoat, since it was June now, and the rains came frequently. Sometimes the streets were flooded. In those days, there were mostly just bicycles, scooters and motorcycles on the roads, not many cars, other than a few government vehicles and delivery trucks. I pedaled fast, proud to bring lunch or dinner to Mom so she didn't have to go outside the hospital and buy food. We closed the store after Daddy got sick, so Mom didn't have much money at that time.

One day at about 11 am, Aunt said, "Get ready, it's almost time to take lunch to your mom and dad." But before I left, my uncle came home from the hospital. He had tears in his eyes and his shoulders were slumped over. He said, "He passed away. Your father passed away." I was shocked. I didn't know what to do. Uncle said, "You should go to the hospital. Bring lunch to your mom."

I got on my bike and pedaled. I was scared, but I didn't cry. Mostly, I was worried.

You see, my father had once been poor, and he knew what it was like to be poor and hungry. He was a healer, skilled in Chinese medicine and diagnosing what part of the body was ill. There were a lot of poor people in our province who worked very hard, like the river porters. They couldn't pay, so my father treated them for free and gave them medicine. Because of this, almost the whole town respected him - even the police and the government. But some wealthy people were jealous. Were those people going to make trouble for us now that he was gone? Were they going to threaten my family?

I got to the hospital around noon. I went into his room, and my dad was covered with a sheet. Mom was crying. I took out the lunch containers, but Mom said she didn't want to eat.

So I just sat next to her. She said, "Do you want to see your daddy for the last time?"

She pulled back the sheet. My daddy looked very still and his eyes were closed. I sat there with my mom while she was crying. We didn't say anything. At about 1pm, she said, "Phu, why don't you go home." She was waiting for people to come and take my father's body away. There was nothing else to do, so I went home. I took a nap, and a couple hours later another uncle came running back from the hospital. He was excited. "Your father is alive!" he said. "He's back alive!" He said that while my mom had been sitting with him, the sheet started moving up and down with Daddy's breath. My mom took off the sheet and talked to him, but he didn't say anything. He touched her arm, and she sat down watching him lie there, breathing.

I went back to the hospital. My father opened his eyes and looked at me. He didn't speak. "Daddy," I said. He touched my hand. He didn't say anything and his eyes started to close. "Daddy, you go ahead and take a nap, I'll just sit here with Mom."

My mom's appetite was back, and she finally ate. After she finished her lunch, my father was snoring. "Why don't you go home and let your father rest?" she said. The hospital smelled like antiseptic and she didn't want me to stay there, it wasn't healthy. So I went back to Grandpa's house. It was about six in the evening.

A couple hours later, my mom came home. She looked very sad and tired. "Why are you home, Mom?" I asked, but I already knew something was wrong. She never left my dad's side. She said, "Daddy spoke after he saw you. He looked at me and said, 'I forgot to say one thing: don't let them leave Vietnam together.' Then, he died."

Three years later, a neighbor from our town was passing by the shrine before sunrise. She saw Mr. Truong cleaning the Buddhist temple, as usual. She waved to him and said, "Hello Mr. Truong!" He said, "I can't talk to you now, very busy. A lot of people are coming here tomorrow." She watched him for a moment, holding his straw broom, cleaning the temple and the lady went home. When the sun came up a few hours later she remembered that Mr. Truong had died. The lady had seen a ghost.

6 LEAVING VIETNAM

Mom told me to go back to Trà-Ôn, so I took a bus the next morning. When I got home, I told my sister that our daddy passed away, and she cried and cried. The next morning, we both went back to Saigon.

That night, Mom said, "Your daddy didn't tell me his wishes before he passed. But while he was sick he said, 'Why do those people who want to leave Vietnam get buried in Vietnam? Why don't they have their bodies burned so their families can take their ashes with them?'" So my mom thought Daddy wanted to be cremated.

Mom and Nora argued. "I don't want to burn my father's body! It's mean!" Nora said. She wanted to bring my father back to Trà-Ôn to be buried there. Mom insisted. "No, he kept mentioning his brother-in-law. He said, 'Why didn't they cremate him if he didn't want to stay in Vietnam?'"

So they decided to ask my father. Mom went out into the hall and burned incense and prayed. She called on my father's spirit by mentioning his name and the time he died. Then she took out two coins. She asked him, "Do you want to go back to Trà-Ôn? Or do you want to be cremated?" She threw the coins up into the air. They landed on the ground, one head and one tail. Then my sister asked. "Dad, I think we should take you back to Trà-Ôn. What do you want?" It came up two tails – my dad was laughing. My mom threw the coins two more times, and they landed the same way – one head and one tail, three times in a row. That meant my mom was right. So my sister agreed. We stayed in Saigon and my dad's body was cremated.

In Vietnamese, my Dad's name was Truong Gia Lam. "Gia" means house and "Lam" means forest. People used to say, "Your dad's heart is as big as a forest."

On the day of my father's funeral, my sister took care of everything. She ran around buying incense and arranging everything for the funeral hall in the back of the hospital. People came from Trà-Ôn to honor him—the whole town, all the neighbors. They said, "He was like a living Buddha. And like Buddha, he passed away." People also came from the countryside, miles away from our town. Farmers and other poor people attended my father's funeral, man of the people who had experienced his kindness. They were crying, "Who's going to help this town now?"

Daddy was only 48 years old. But in our culture, we believe that good people die young. In Buddhism, we're not worried about living a long life. If we die early, we go to heaven early. Good people die early to pay off debts from a previous life.

The Buddhist monk told my mother, "Life punishes us. Life is suffering. It is our discipline. Death and heaven are relief from suffering. Your husband's punishment has ended.

He finished his suffering early, and now he has gone to heaven." That made my mother feel a little better.

On the day of the funeral, we finally received a letter from my brother David. My mom's cousin stood by my dad's ashes and read the letter out loud. "Hey big cousin," he said. My mom was crying. "Only three nights and two days after our boat left Vietnam, we reached the Malaysian refugee camp called Tanga. We are all safe, and I am thinking of going to the USA."

The USA. When I heard that David was going to the USA, I got excited again.

After the funeral, my mom, sister, and I returned to Trà-Ôn. I asked my mom, "Mom, can I go to the USA to look for my older brother?"

"No, you are only 12 years old. You're too young to go by yourself," she said. But a few days later, Mom heard a rumor in the neighborhood that made her change her mind. The Communists were getting ready to invade Cambodia. They said it was necessary to protect the country, but in reality they were just greedy. They were looking for boys 14 and older to join the army. My mom got scared. She knew that if we waited until I was 14, I could get arrested. It was better to go now.

After the Communists came, my dad had purchased a little rice field just outside the town to make sure we still had some property, in case they took our homes. My mom had learned how to cultivate rice when she was a girl in China, so she took care of the field and sold some of the rice.

Mom started making plans. She decided to fool the Communists into thinking we were poor and that we didn't have any money to escape. She sold grilled squid and fish that she cooked over charcoal and she made gin from rice and sold it at night to the neighbors.

She closed her little bar at midnight and got up at 4am, walked to the ferry and bought fresh fruit to sell, too. At night, she would tune in to ABC France radio and listen to reports on the refugee situation. It was illegal to listen to news in Vietnamese from other countries, so it was very risky; but she listened to her little radio with the volume turned way down low. She got news about refugees and the boats. How many boats perished? How many reached the Philippines? If the Communists found out she was listening to this station, they could easily put her in jail and take the house. They were always looking for reasons.

Mom waited a few weeks. No one knew what she was planning, not even me. When she had enough money, and everything was ready, she said, "If you really want to go look for your brother, it is OK." I was ready. "Yes! I want to go," I said.

Mom had heard that it was easiest to leave from South Vietnam, near the South China Sea.

"Go to Kiên Gian," she said. "You'll see a lot of people there. Follow them, and you'll find a boat. Your sister will go a few months later. I will stay at home, just in case something goes wrong and you have to come home."

At that time, there were a lot of swindlers who promised you a place on a boat. They took your money and it all turned out to be a scam. Whole families paid for passage and left their houses behind only to find that there was no boat. When they returned, Communist soldiers had already occupied their homes. Now the families had no money and no home to return to.

I was her youngest son, and I was going alone. Nobody knew I was planning to leave, not even my uncles. If anyone found out, it could put us all in jeopardy. At that time, the

Communists were coming around and asking almost every day, "Where are your children?" So, it was better if no one knew the truth.

"You have to promise me that you will take care of yourself and stay away from trouble," she said.

"I promise." I did not want to let my mom down.

❖

I got ready to leave my hometown of Trà-Ôn. Mom gave me enough money for the ferry and the bus, and there was 200,000 Vietnam dong (about 10 US dollars then) left over, enough to buy food for a week or two. I took the ferry to Cần-Thơ, and then rode a bus about four and a half hours south. I stopped at a city called Rach Gia in Kiên Gian province on the Mekong Delta. Then I took another bus to Rach Soi. From there, I didn't know which way to go. So I waited and watched.

I stayed near the buses. After a few hours, I saw a group of people carrying suitcases. I wasn't sure if these people were locals or tourists, so I paid attention to what they did at the bus terminal. I waited and waited. More buses came in and more people. I saw a group of people with a kid about my age, and I felt those people were looking for a boat. So, I went up to the boy and pretended that I knew him.

"Hey, are you coming back? You've been gone for a long time," I said. He just looked at me and said nothing. "Don't you remember? We're in the same class in Ming Middle School?" (I just made up a name. "Ming" means 'smart' in Vietnamese).

"I don't know you. I'm just coming from Saigon," the boy answered.

The boy's parents pulled him away and said, "Stay away from him." That's when I knew, *this is the right group*. They are scared of strangers, because most of the people running away are carrying a lot of money – their entire fortunes – and they are frightened of being robbed.

"Are you sure?" I continued, hoping to get more information. "You know – my big house is down there," and I pointed to the town, wanting to make them think I was rich. In the countryside, there aren't any schools, so rich families always sent their kids to Saigon to go to school.

The rich people were the ones that could afford to leave the country first, because they could pay the boatmen with gold. The price was ten 24K gold bars per person, about $3,750 U.S. dollars at that time. Kids under 15 years old paid half – five gold bars. Passengers usually didn't know the owner of the boat and they only dealt with the middleman. Each group had it's own middleman, and once he made enough money, he would find a way to get his own family out of the country, too. Most of the middlemen were making money hand over fist.

I followed this family to find their middleman. The middleman took the group for a ride in a small canoe all the way into the deep countryside. I paid my fare and took the canoe, too. We rode for about 20-30 minutes and in the late afternoon we arrived at a very small village called Tà Niên on the Mekong River. All around the village were pineapple fields, and the people there were strong and healthy farmers who grew pineapples for a living.

By this time, the village was full of people waiting for boats. It was profitable for the villagers, because all of these people needed food and a place to stay for a while – sometimes one to two weeks, or a month or more, depending on how soon the boat owner was ready to go. Sometimes they had to wait for enough people to go. Every single house was booked up in this village with people waiting. The landlords charged high prices – about 500,000 Vietnamese dong a week (25 US dollars then) including three meals a day.

I didn't have money for rent, so I found an old abandoned school. The walls were crumbling and the roof was full of holes. Just like my school, bombs had destroyed it during the war. It smelled terrible, but I had no other choice, so I stayed in the broken-down school.

At night, when it was very dark, I looked up from where I was sleeping and could see the stars through the holes in the roof. I could hear the mosquitoes singing. The floor was so dirty and disgusting, I was afraid to lie down on it. People sometimes came in and used the abandoned school as a toilet. I was scared of rats coming during the night. So I just sat in the corner, and leaned against a wall while I slept. When the wind blew, the windows made noise. But that was OK, because I didn't want to sleep too deeply. Sometimes boats left in the middle of the night and I had to keep alert.

I was a little scared on the first night. It was very cold and wet and I didn't have a blanket – only two long-sleeved shirts and two pairs of long pants. The second night I learned to put on all my clothes to keep the mosquitoes from biting me. Then, I found some old newspapers and stuffed them inside my clothes to keep warm.

I slept in this school for three days, and on the third day I got really sick. My body got very weak, my lips turned black, and my vision got blurry. I didn't know what had happened, but I knew I was very ill. There was no hospital or doctor in this village, and I was so scared. I kept thinking that I was going to die. But I had promised my mom I would take care of myself. *I can't die*, I thought. *I have to be strong and fight for my life.*

I went to a house that was close to the school and knocked on the door. The owner of the house, a very tall and muscular man, opened the door.

"Oh, my God, child, what is wrong with you?" he asked, bringing me inside his home. "What did you eat and what did you drink?"

"I ate my sandwich that I brought three days ago, and I drank the water in the big ceramic pot in the back of the school," I said.

"No wonder!" the man said, "The people in this village drink only boiled water. You can't drink water like that. You got poisoned."

The man's name was Mr. Han. He fed me plain rice soup with lots of chili peppers and an egg yolk. He made me eat a lot of peppers, and my tongue started to burn. My lips swelled and my eyes started watering. There was so much noise inside my ears – boom, boom, boom. After five or six hours, my body broke out into a sweat, and my shirt got very wet with what looked like black ink. The poison inside my body had been released. I started to feel hungry and thirsty. Mr. Han smiled.

"You are very lucky," he said. "If you had come two days later, you might have died from the poison." I thanked him for helping me. He saved my life.

After that, Mr. Han let me stay in his house for free. It was a small close-knit community and all the neighbors were very kind and knew each other very well. They were nice to all the refugees, treating everyone like family. It was very peaceful there. I never heard anyone argue the whole time. They were always sharing food.

Every day I went with Mr. Han to his pineapple fields to help. I watered the pineapples, carried things for him, sprayed pesticides or hunted rats. We ate the big farm rats with clear blue eyes that got fat from eating off the fields – not the dirty ones with red eyes that eat garbage from the city. The rats tasted good. I kept helping him, waiting for whenever a boat would be ready to go.

Six months passed. Boats came and went, but always in secret, so we only heard about them after they left. Finally a neighbor came and told Mr. Han, "We have a boat landing here in a couple days. It's coming to pick up passengers." So, Mr. Han said, "Phu! It's time. Get ready to go."

The boat came on the afternoon of April 23, 1979. I waited and watched while they loaded their water and food. Then the captain of the boat started to take a roll call of the passengers, family by family. Finally Mr. Lam's name was called.

I had been watching Mr. Lam's family for six months, ever since I followed them to the island in the little canoe. I picked Mr. Lam's family because he had grandparents and four kids in his group. I used a trick that Mr. Han had taught me, because he knew I had no money: he said, "When you get to the boat, it will be full of people. Very crowded and confused. While they call roll, you can sneak in when they're not paying attention."

I went up to Mr. Lam's family and pretended that I worked for the boat. I told Mr. Lam, "I will help you carry your luggage." In the confusion, Mr. Lam thought I was with the boat crew, and the boat owners thought that I was with Mr. Lam's family. So, just like that, I went on board, because everyone was in a hurry. They wanted to leave as soon as possible.

It was a small, light green, wooden fishing boat, only 19 meters long, four and a half meters wide. They had fixed it up to transport refugees. That meant they had removed all the fishing equipment to make room for 260 men, women, and children to sit in the boat like sardines. We couldn't even move. If you stood up, you would lose your spot. The hold had no windows, the walls of the boat looked very old and worn, and there was a very bad, fishy smell. I sat down next to a pregnant woman.

When everything was loaded and ready, the boat started to leave Vietnam. It was a little after sunset, and the captain said, "If we're lucky we'll be in Malaysia in three days and two nights. But it's not guaranteed." Our plan was to go to a Malaysian refugee camp. I felt excited. I was dreaming of chocolate, Coca-Cola, and of finding my brother.

"Boat People"
Refugees from Vietnam on a boat very similar to Phu's

7 PIRATES

The boat owner, his family, relatives and friends, and the VIPs who paid extra gold stayed on the top deck. There were a lot of people up there. There was no cover for the deck and it was very cold at night. When the boat hit the big waves, they all got very wet.

Meanwhile, I was underneath in the hold, where it was very hot and everyone was sweaty and could not move. I was just wearing my shorts and a T-shirt, I didn't have any shoes, or food, or money. I just carried a clean T-shirt with me in a plastic bag. The pregnant lady was sitting on my left, and an old lady on my right. After a couple hours, the pregnant lady was already sick and lying down.

The first night wasn't bad because we were still close to land. But by the next morning, we were in the open sea. The boat began to roll left and right. People started to get scared, screaming that our load was too heavy. People were crying and whimpering that they wanted to go back because they thought the boat would sink and they were going to die. They regretted leaving.

The captain of the boat yelled, "Everybody quiet. It's too late for regrets. We have to go on, because we are looking for our freedom." Everybody calmed down and balance was restored to the boat.

After a few hours, just before midnight, people got tired and some went to sleep. It was so hot and humid in the hold that it was very hard to breathe. Luckily, I don't get seasick, so I didn't throw up. But the lady sitting next to me threw up on me several times, right on my T-shirt. She got my body all wet and stinky, but I was afraid to stand up because I would lose my spot. So I changed into my one extra T-shirt and put up with the smell.

Then the people on the opposite side of the boat got sick and started throwing up, too. Now the boat smelled really bad, like rotten fish mixed with vomit, sweat, and heat. That made everybody sick: kids were crying because they couldn't breathe, and then the boat started to roll left and right again and again.

Early the next morning, everyone on deck became so excited. We could hear yelling above us: "There are two boats following us! Oh, we're getting rescued!"

The captain announced to everyone, "We're in the Gulf of Thailand now. If this is a commercial ship or a military ship from any country, then we are lucky. We will be safe and sound because they will pick us up. Or at least they can help us, and take us to their country."

Everybody stood up, shouting. Some people started burning their clothes to draw attention from the large boats. I couldn't see anything from inside the hold, but I was hoping that the boats were from the US Navy. Then I could find my brother faster.

These two big boats were coming closer and closer. We were all waiting with lots of hope.

Then I heard, "Oh my god, pirates, pirates!" The people on deck yelled down to us – "Hey, pirates are coming! Watch out!" People started panicking. They stood up and started hiding their gold and valuables. The captain said, "Everybody calm down!" but it was too late. The boat was rocking with fear.

Those big boats kept coming closer and closer. They were three times longer and one and a half times taller than our boat, and a lot faster. Our boat was too small to run away, but the captain tried. They chased us for almost an hour. Finally, one of the pirate boats was on our front right side and the other was on the back left. We couldn't do anything to escape. If they crossed us, we would be overturned and we would all die. We were trapped. We would just have to obey them and give them whatever they wanted.

Now they were close enough to see. There were more than 20 big-muscled guys, with dark skin and dragons and tigers tattooed all over their bare chests. Their faces were painted with many different colors. They carried big knives, machetes, axes, and long wooden sticks. They were Thai pirates.

They jumped onto our boat and started to beat the men and older boys. The leader stayed on his boat, watching, while another pirate pointed a handgun at us. It was clear that if anyone tried to escape, they would be shot.

Passengers started yelling, "Get down, get down!" to avoid being beaten. I curled up into a little ball, leaning into the guy sitting next to me. I was scared, but I kept my eyes open to see what was happening.

After they finished beating up the men, they started searching for money, gold, and diamonds. The captain of the boat gave them four suitcases of gold bars. The pirates searched every single person on the boat. They took watches, bracelets, necklaces and earrings. They got a lot of jewelry. One girl had a diamond ring that she could not get off, so one of the pirates cut off her finger with a machete. Someone wrapped her hand in a T-shirt to stop the bleeding while she cried in pain.

When the pirates came down into the hold, a young passenger about 20 years old ripped open a package of bean cakes. He tore apart a cake, looking for something – then he swallowed a diamond. The pirates saw him, and then they checked everyone's food. After they found what they wanted, they dumped all our food and water into the ocean. The father of the boy who ate the diamond started yelling at him. "What are we going to do now? We have no water or food!" Everybody was whining and screaming and praying to God, "Help us, help us!"

The pirates knew what they were doing. They were professionals. They went down to the engine room and broke apart the engine and found more gold hidden there.

Once they had found all of the jewels and gold, they started to gang rape the women and young girls.

They raped two sisters, aged 14 and 15 years old. The pirates put them over the railing, took their clothes off and took turns. The girls' mother went crazy. She took her own clothes off and screamed, "Leave the girls alone! Do anything you want to me. They are too young for you!" So, they raped the mother as well as the girls.

One of the pirates spoke Chinese. He taunted the girls, who were hurt and bleeding. He said, "Give me a baby boy so he can be mean, like me."

Another pirate held a knife to the young pregnant woman sitting next to me. Two other pirates held her arms and the lead pirate pulled off her pants and raped her violently. The woman's husband tried to protect her, so they hit him on the head with an axe. Another pirate stabbed him, and his blood exploded all over me. After they were finished raping, the pirates left.

Everyone was crying and screaming. The pregnant woman's husband was dead. After the pirates left, I noticed a machete. It was long, maybe 12 inches, with a curved blade and a steel handle, laying a few inches front of me. Instinctively, I quickly covered the knife with some ripped clothes that were lying around and hid it behind me.

The pregnant woman started banging her head on the side of the boat and crying. "How can I live? I don't want my baby to grow up without a father." The captain and a few other men dumped her husband's body into the ocean. She wanted to jump into the ocean after him, but an old lady calmed her. "You have to be strong and live for your baby," she told her. The pregnant woman just sat there in her arms, crying and rocking.

In the middle of the night, when no one was watching, the pregnant woman jumped into the ocean. We didn't know she was gone until the morning.

I had the machete, but forgot about it because we had another problem. The captain and the mechanic couldn't fix the engine. They tried and tried, but five hours later the engine still had no power. It was getting dark. We all knew we were going to die. The boat was just floating along with the ocean current. We hoped for a miracle to save us, but on all four sides we saw nothing but water. All we heard were waves. The babies were crying, and the injured people were moaning.

After that, I wanted to go to the upper deck to get away from the misery and get some air. It was a mess; there was blood everywhere. I tried to go up, but a guy on top stepped on my head and pushed me back down into the hold. I got very mad.

I waited until the sun set and went back up to the deck. I waited and waited, and finally saw the guy standing by the railing, smoking. He was around 30 years old and traveling alone, like me. Oh boy, I thought to myself. This guy needs to be taught a lesson. I jumped over to the railing and grabbed him around the neck. I pulled us both toward the ocean.

"What are you doing?" he cried.

"We are all going to die anyway, so leave me alone or we're going to die together in the ocean now, OK?" I said, wrapping my arms around his neck and pulling him toward the railing.

"Stop it, stop it, I can't swim!" he pleaded. His face turned green and he was shaking all over. I let him go and said, "Stop picking on me."

He apologized and volunteered to take my place down in the hold for a while. I said OK, and he went below. I stayed up on the deck and breathed in the fresh sea air.

The next morning we were all tired, hungry, and thirsty. Nobody knew what to do. When the sun came up at six in the morning, somebody yelled, "Another boat is coming toward us!" We were all happy and thought, this boat will help us. Now we will be saved! We screamed and waved our hands. Again, we burnt some clothes to make smoke signals. But when the boat came closer, we saw the black skull flag.

"Pirates again!" the captain yelled. "Ladies and children, go down into the hold!" They went down, and I was left on top with the other young men.

This time, it was only one boat but it was twice as big as ours. It had a powerful engine and was coming at us really fast. As it neared, we saw two big guys standing in the bow with their arms crossed. Other pirates were standing behind them, holding big knives and long shotguns or rifles strapped across their chest. We still had no engine. No way to escape.

All of us men and boys were standing there looking at them. I guess they thought we were ready to fight them, but we were already exhausted.

When they got close enough, we heard them speaking Thai. One of them was pointing at us with the rope. I was standing there, and I realized, "Oh, he needs someone to hold the rope." Then I got an idea. He threw the rope over and everyone looked at the rope on the deck of the boat. I grabbed the rope and held it for them. Everyone looked at me.

About 10 huge, dark men jumped onto our boat. Most of them had painted faces. Some wore masks. They looked very mean. They had huge muscles and tattoos, and a lot of guns. They started beating up the guys on the boat. Then they pointed at us to sit down. There wasn't anything we could do. I just stood there, holding the rope, and they didn't beat me. That's why I grabbed the rope – I was hoping if I helped them they wouldn't hurt me.

They searched all the passengers' bodies, but found nothing. They got so angry – they had come a day too late and there wasn't much left. But still they tried very hard to find anything valuable. This group had a lot of experience. They went underneath the hull of the boat and found two boxes of gold near the propeller. Now they were a little happier. They came back to the boat and checked everybody again, especially all the ladies. They made them take off all their clothes to make sure they weren't hiding money. They found some American dollars. Then they started laughing and having fun. They went down into the hold and raped, over and over again.

The same teenage sisters were raped again. The mother tried to stop them, and the pirates beat her. She was badly injured.

For Asian people at that time, virginity was very important. The sisters couldn't stand it. They had been raped three or four times by each group of pirates. How could they get married now? How could they ever have a happy life? They felt they had nothing to live for.

The pirates were only there about 30 minutes. Then they came up and gave me a can of Coca-Cola and left. *I'm not going to share this with anyone*, I thought. I drank it quickly. It was warm and sweet. Everyone hated me.

After they left, people had had bloody noses, broken teeth and bruises. They were checking each other, asking about their injuries and tending to their wounds.

Near sundown, the two sisters held hands, stood on the railing of the boat and jumped off into the stormy sea. The captain of the boat jumped in and tried to save them, but they pushed him away. The girls couldn't swim, and they sank little by little. There was nothing he could do, so the captain swam back to the boat.

We looked over the railing into the huge, rolling waves, but we couldn't see the two sisters.

Later, in the middle of the night, the mother of the girls went mad. She began screaming, "I can't live without my girls! Kill me so I can go with my girls!" Then, somehow she climbed up over the broken wood and luggage and jumped over the railing, yelling "Kids, wait for me. We go together. We die together!" Everyone was so tired and helpless that they let her go. Nobody tried to save her.

By noon, the sun was so hot and we were all suffering from thirst and hunger. We were worried about food and water. You could hear the kids crying and the old people praying to God. One old man said, "We are all going to die, so I'll kill myself and become a god, to save all of you," and he jumped into the ocean. His wife jumped with him, leaving their two kids and 14 grandchildren behind on the boat. Their two sons had been beaten really badly by the pirates and could do nothing to save their parents. The eldest of the 14 grandchildren was only 11 years old.

After several hours, it got dark, windy, and very cold. We prayed for rain, but it didn't come. We had no engine power and the boat was very dark. A lot of people were sick and the injured were moaning. The next morning when the sun rose, the water was very calm and we were all hoping for help. But no help came.

We were all really hungry and thirsty and didn't know what to do. An ex-navy captain was on board. He was a medic, but we called him "Doctor." He told us to collect matches and lighters and light a fire to boil seawater. He said we could take turns licking the condensed steam off the lid to survive.

We made a fire in the back of the boat, where there was a little stove. The babies and old people had priority and then the rest of us took turns licking the steam from the lid of the pot. All 250+ passengers did this all day. Our boat was just drifting, and sometime sea horses and flying fish would jump onto the boat. We put them into the pot and cooked them, letting the kids and old people eat them first.

The next day was the fourth day and the sea was still really calm until the afternoon. We saw another boat, and this time we didn't expect help. We didn't give them a signal. We had lost hope. Whatever would come would come.

It was another group of Thai pirates. They circled our boat three times and could see that we had already been beaten and robbed. I jumped right to the front of the boat and waved my hand to signal them to throw the rope over. They threw me the rope and I grabbed it. The other passengers on the boat scowled at me and gave me dirty looks. Someone asked why I was helping them. "Oh, are you a professional ass-kisser?"

"Did you get beaten up last time?" I said.

"Yes," the man said.

"That's why I am helping them, so I don't get beaten up!" He just laughed.

This time there were about 15 of them. They also had huge physiques, with faces painted like the others.

But these guys looked like accidental pirates: They had no guns – just lots of knives, axes, and sharpened wooden chopsticks. When they jumped onto our boat, they could see that we were all exhausted and had no fight left in us. They didn't beat anybody.

One of the pirates could speak English, and he talked to the captain of the boat in English. Then they went down to the hold and pulled all the women to the top of the boat and started to rape them. One of the men on our boat became hysterical and started shouting while clutching a tube of toothpaste, "I'll give you diamonds if you stop raping my wife!" The pirates punched him and took the tube of toothpaste. They opened it and found it was full of diamonds.

After that, the pirates collected all the toothpaste from everybody and took everybody's shoes and cut them up, finding more jewels and American dollars. They took all our shoes and belts, and searched our clothes to see if money was hidden inside the lining and hems. After that they went back to raping the ladies. They finally left after six hours.

On the fifth day nothing happened. We just sat on the boat waiting for help. We were still floating in the Gulf of Thailand. The seahorses were keeping us alive, thank God, by occasionally hopping into our boat. We saw other boats come up and circle us. They looked like more pirates, but they left because they could see we had already been robbed. They left and never helped us.

In the late afternoon when the sun was almost going down, one of the old men died from the stress. The captain dumped his body into the ocean.

The captain was as exhausted as the rest of us, but he was still the leader of the group.

"The seahorses aren't enough to keep all of us alive," he announced. "Whenever anyone else dies, we will have to eat the body."

People started crying and going crazy. We looked at each other with eyes of suspicion. Then, everyone went quiet. The boat kept rocking. I thought, *hey, if you're going to eat my body, I'd rather jump into the ocean.* But I'd already promised my mother that I wouldn't die. For the first time, I started to cry.

On the sixth day, we were still taking turns licking the condensed steam and eating the seahorses whole, even the bones. It was so hot: 100-degree days and 80-degree nights. Other than the steam, we had no water. Then a baby, maybe two years old, died. The mother of the baby was crying and would not let the baby go.

"It's my baby," she cried. "You can't eat my baby's organs!" She went all the way to the front of the boat. She found a big knife and held it up, shouting, "No one can eat my baby!" We left her alone, and no one paid attention to her all the way into the afternoon.

When people began talking about eating each other, I remembered the machete. *No one is going to eat me*, I thought. And if I had to, I already knew which guy I was going to eat – the one who I fought with and who kept picking on me.

At five in the afternoon, we saw a big ship coming, closer and closer. We had no hope left. But the ship came closer, and we didn't see a black flag. Instead, we saw a white and red colored flag. We started to think it was a commercial ship. It came closer and closer and it was the Singapore Navy! It was not a really big ship, but it was at least two or three times the size of ours. We wept happy tears!

The captain of our boat and the man who we called Doctor shouted up to the Singapore Navy in English. Two of them, one who could speak Chinese and one who could speak English, came onto our boat. They lowered water and food to us – bread, canned food, Spam, and crackers. And I saw Coca-Cola, chocolate, and cigarettes! Everyone tried to grab something. I grabbed some bread and cigarettes.

After that, they brought us some of their own clothes, like shorts and T-shirts. We used them to cover the old people and the women. It was a miracle, and we all thanked God. They talked with our captain for over half an hour.

The captain of the Navy ship said, "By our rules, we cannot take you to Singapore. But we can tow your boat closer to land, probably close to a Malaysian refugee camp." We said, OK, whatever; we were grateful to get any help at all.

Around eight o'clock that night, they slowly started to tow our boat. We began to feel a little energized, with a little food in our bellies and hope for survival. I looked out at the ocean and I watched the waves go up and down. I understood that people's lives are like that – up and down, the ocean's way.

Everyone started talking about their futures now, saying, "I'll work very hard when I get to a foreign country. And I'll send my money back to Vietnam, because my wife and kids are waiting for me." Some women said, "Me too," because their husbands had been South Vietnam soldiers fighting the Communists, and now were prisoners in reeducation camps. Everybody was talking about what country they planned to go to. Of course, everybody wanted to go to the USA. We were all tired, but finally we felt safe and relieved. We began to sleep after a while.

The Singapore Navy towed our boat for one day and one night. The next morning somebody yelled, "Hey, where's the navy ship?" It was gone. They had untied the towrope early in the morning and we could see birds and trees very far away.

Now, we needed to worry about how to get to land and had no idea how to do it. All we could do was pray to God and wait for a miracle again. At least we were not scared of the pirates anymore. We felt stronger, knowing we were close to land. So we waited and waited. The ocean waves were big, and the current was running pretty strong. The wind was pretty strong too, and it was carrying us toward the shore. Somebody burned some clothing to try to get someone's attention from land, but nobody came.

The food and water that the Singapore Navy ship gave us ran out, so we resorted to boiling seawater again. Everybody's lips were cracked and dry and hurting. A lot of kids were crying from thirst and hunger, especially the babies.

A toddler sitting across from me, said, "Mama, when can I see Daddy? How much longer do we have to wait to see Daddy?"

"Has the baby ever seen her daddy?" someone asked.

"Yeah, when the baby was born," the mother said. "On April 30, 1975." That was "Independence Day," when the Communists won the battle. The father of the baby was a surgeon with the South Vietnamese Army, and, like many other soldiers, got sent to a reeducation camp.

When the sun came up, the heat was making people very hot, thirsty, and hungry again. We boiled seawater again and took turns licking the steam. Then somebody got an idea. "We should break up the wooden railing and use it to paddle the boat to shore," Everybody agreed, so we helped tear off the railing and began paddling the boat little by little. The boat was very heavy so it didn't really move, but it was better than doing nothing and just sitting there.

Then about 10 men jumped into the ocean and started pushing the boat from behind and kicking. Another 10 men jumped into the water and pulled the boat with the rope left by the Singapore Navy. It all helped a little – and at least it kept us from floating further from shore. We keep trying and trying. We took turns pushing and pulling the boat in the water. After many hours, the boat did move closer to land. The captain said, "OK, whoever can swim, start swimming toward land. And we'll see how much more we can push the boat and get it close enough for people to walk onto shore."

The captain of the boat and some guys swam toward the shore to check how far it was, but it was still pretty far. The rope was not long enough to drag it ashore, so they came back to the boat and got another idea: get all our clothes – shirts and pants and anything left – and tie them onto the rope as an extension to make the rope longer. It took about two hours for us to collect enough clothing to tie it into a long rope. We thought it should be enough to pull the boat ashore.

I jumped into the water with the others to help pull the boat in. Finally, with all of our efforts, the boat touched the sand and we were ashore. By the time we landed it was almost dark – about 6:30pm. We had been at sea for one week. The day we landed was April 30, 1979 – Independence Day.

The children and elderly had priority. We helped them hold on to the rope as they walked ashore. Family members carried their old relatives and young children on their backs. After everybody was safely on land, we worried about the Malaysian government forcing us back onto the ocean. So the captain said, "Let's tear down the boat and make sure it sinks." We pulled it apart until we had no boat left. Now, the Malaysian government could not push us out.

So here we were safely on shore, finally! But now we faced another problem: we'd landed right near a Malaysian Army base. About 30 soldiers were running out to greet us with M16s and hand grenades.

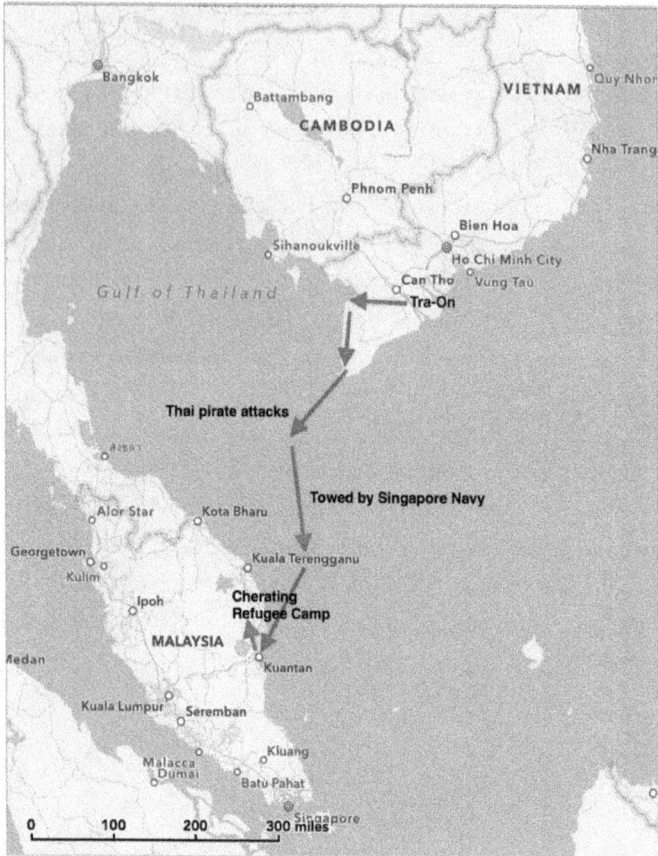

Phu Truong's journey, 1979

8 FREEDOM CAMP, FREEDOM JAIL

We had landed at Kuantan, a Malaysian Army base. Even though we were injured and exhausted, the army acted as though we were coming ashore to attack them because they sent out soldiers armed with guns and hand grenades. They pushed us with their loaded M16s, and told us to sit down on the ground.

We were weak and tired, and they were so mean. We couldn't communicate. None of us could speak Malaysian – but they had a Chinese-Malaysian soldier who could understand us.

"Where are you coming from? Why are you here?" he asked.

"We're hungry," I said in Mandarin. I was very scared and shaking.

"Everybody lie down on the ground – children under 18 on one side, seniors and women on the other side," the soldiers said.

They asked the captain for a list of passengers, but it had been lost along with the boat, so he had to go around and identify everyone. After that was finally done, it was already past 10pm.

The Malaysian Army now realized that we were really refugees and they started to help us a little bit. We told them that we were hungry and thirsty. They called back to their base and brought us a little food, sweet buns, and some water and Coca-Cola.

We stayed on the beach overnight. The sand was wet and there was no protection from the cold wind. It started to rain hard, and we had nothing for shelter. We were already wet from wading ashore, and we had very little clothing left after making our towrope. We all stayed awake. Nobody could sleep. Kids were crying so loudly. Everybody huddled close to each other around a big tree. There were about 250 of us left.

By the next morning, one old man had passed away from exposure to the rain and cold. We still had no support.

A few hours later – around 10 o'clock in the morning – three vans and a car with the Red Cross insignia drove up. Caucasian workers gave us food, water, and some clothing, and blankets. We asked the Red Cross people to bury the old man who passed away. They put him in a plastic bag and took him away to be buried.

The rain was still pouring and it was very windy, so the Red Cross workers provided three tents and helped us set them up on the beach. We stayed inside the tents where at least we got some protection from the rain. We ate crackers and sweet breads, and we had water, coffee, Coke, and cigarettes. On the second night, we were afraid that more people would die. A lot of the kids were sick. The Red Cross hadn't taken anyone to the hospital; they just gave us some medicine, like

Tylenol. I told myself, "A better day will come." At least that's what I hoped.

On the morning of the third day, the rain finally stopped and the sun came out. I saw a lot of buses coming, and I knew they were coming for us. In fact, they brought us more supplies – clothes, water, food and medicine. Around midday, they brought more buses and said they would take us to a shelter.

We drove a long way. After about four hours, we arrived at an abandoned school. We were allowed to stay inside the building, but nobody could go outside. The Malaysian police patrolled the perimeter of the school and prevented us from going outside. It felt like we were in jail.

Now we had the problem of the restroom. The line was very long and the restroom was very busy, all day and all night long. Now that we were finally getting real food and water, everybody really needed to go. The school restroom was too small for 250 people, so everybody had to hold it for several days.

The school had no electrical power and the government gave us candles and kerosene lamps. We didn't have enough toilet tissue, but the Malaysian people who lived in the neighborhood came over and gave us more candles, matches, and toilet paper.

The old school was in pretty good shape, and the young kids and the old people slept in the classrooms. However, it was awfully hot and there were a lot of mosquitoes at night, so we gathered dry leaves and made smoky fires to keep the mosquitoes away. Every day the neighbors came around the perimeter of the school and tried to sell us things like toothpaste and toothbrushes, food, and cigarettes. But we had no money left to spend. The neighbors offered to buy our jewelry, but no one had any.

I met another Chinese-Malaysian soldier that I could speak Mandarin with. I asked him to send a letter back to my mom in Vietnam. I couldn't write or read – I could only write my Chinese name. So I drew a picture of the boat on the beach with some trees and birds and the sun so that she would know I was safe on land. He promised he would send it for me. I hoped my mom would understand my picture.

Mom got the letter. Before she even looked at the picture, her tears had made the paper wet. Later that day, she burned the letter so the government wouldn't find it.

After living in the school for a week, we were transferred to a small refugee camp called Cherating in Pahang, 30 km north of Kuantan. The population of this camp was about 8,000 or 9,000 people. It was an area of about six square blocks, a tent city with a 10-foot chain link fence around it, located right by the beach.

At first they put up enough big canopy tents to house one per family per tent, but then too many people came so they had to put four families in each tent. Each tent divided into four sections left just 200 square feet for each family. There were no interior walls, so families separated their spaces by hanging blankets or piling up cardboard boxes to make walls. I slept on the ground on a piece of plastic with a cardboard box for a pillow. This was just before the rainy season in June and July, and when the rains did come, the tents didn't protect us. The rain came in right through the cardboard walls so some people hung plastic tarps up on the sides.

Seven to ten Malaysian soldiers carrying M16 rifles guarded the perimeter of the camp 24 hours a day. We called our new camp, "Freedom Jail." The Malaysian soldiers let us out once a week, when they opened the gate and led us single-file down to the ocean to swim. From 10am until 5pm that day, everybody bathed in the ocean. The camp was so dirty and there was trash everywhere on the ground. Nobody really cleaned up, and only a few people who still had money could afford to buy soap. Almost everyone had developed open sores and rashes in these conditions, so we couldn't wait to get out of the camp to bathe in the healing salt water.

Fresh water for cooking and drinking was piped in twice a day – two hours in the morning and two hours in the evening. People stood in line for an hour or more to collect the water from six little hoses. Some residents who had been living there for a while had accumulated extra buckets and could get a lot more water. But more recent refugees often had nothing to carry the water in, and almost every day there would be fights in the water line. The people with more buckets would sometimes try to sell water to people who had no money.

When men fought they would be arrested and taken "to the sands," where they were tied up, stripped and left to burn on the hot sand for a number of hours. It didn't matter who was right or who was wrong – any fighters would be punished. This stopped the fighting over water and made the camp safer, but the fighting went on their records, and those people could never go to the USA.

There were groups of single men in the camp who had nothing to live for; many of them had watched pirates kill their loved ones. Others were wild to begin with, and a lot of these single men became violent and formed gangs. Other refugees joined for protection. Because they had become violent, no country would agree to take these men, and their files went to the bottom of the pile. Some of them had been living in the camp for over a year and a half.

If you had money, you could trade a pack of cigarettes or give $1 (or 2 Malaysian Ringgit) to some of the gang members in exchange for three or four places closer in the water line.

In the back of the camp there were separate bathing facilities for men and women next to an aboveground concrete tank. The women would stand on one side and the men on the other side, scooping water out of the tank and pouring it over themselves to bathe.

Behind these baths the Malaysians had dug latrines, 10 for the men and 10 for the women. These were really bad; they smelled horrible. You couldn't look down or you'd get sick. It was 90-100°F every day and you'd get a headache from breathing the putrid air. Most people would smoke cigarettes when they went in to help cover the stench. Or, they would use the latrines at night, when there was a little more privacy and the cool night wind would rise up and blow away the stench, making it more tolerable to breathe.

Every day at 4pm, the supply truck brought fresh vegetables. There was always enough for everyone. Then, once every three days, the canned food truck would come around with sardines, white rice, and canned vegetables like beans and peas. Sometimes there were tins of beef or pork, but only twice a month. How much you got depended on how many people were in your family: each person got two kilos of rice, five cans of sardines, three cans of peas, and sometimes two cans of corned beef or two cans of pork. I remember this, because I was always hungry. I was a big eater, and for me, it was never enough. Sometimes I would share meals with a big family with lots of kids. Finally, I could get enough to eat.

Mrs. Nguyen and her mother lived across from me in our big tent. Her husband, an ex-Vietnamese soldier, was detained in a Communist reeducation camp. The first day I got supplies,

I had a can of vegetables but no can opener. I went over to her and asked, "How do you open this?"

"You just come in?" she asked.

"Yes, I'm by myself," I said.

"Why don't we cook for him?" Mrs. Nguyen's mother said. Her mother was old and thin, and she didn't eat too much.

"Can you carry water for us?" asked Mrs. Nguyen.

"Yes!" I said. This looked like a good deal.

Mrs. Nguyen was in her mid-30s and I called her "Sister Nguyen" as a sign of respect. I called her mom, "Auntie."

They had two plastic buckets. Every day I took the buckets and got into the water line. I filled them up in the morning and night and carried the heavy buckets back to the tent. I also carried wood for cooking. I shared all of my food rations with them and they cooked for me. That way, we became friends.

There was nothing to do in the camp. So every morning I sat outside the tent and watched representatives from all the different countries pass by. They were from the USA and Canada, Australia, Germany, France, England, Switzerland, Denmark, Holland, Belgium, Sweden, Japan, and a few more countries.

They said, "Good morning" to each other, so that is the first English phrase that I learned. I knew "Good morning" was a greeting, but in the countryside, we just say, "Hey," or "Hi," so I had no idea what it meant. After that I said, "Good morning" no matter what time of day it was. The second phrase I learned was, "Sir, you have a cigarette?" Once in a while the workers would give me one if I asked them as they passed by.

Once a week the country representatives interviewed us, family by family, to see who was qualified to enter their country. They asked us about our families and if we had relatives in their countries. If we were offered a spot, we could choose to go to that representative's country or not.

To go to the USA, "A" candidates had first priority. "A" candidates were those who had a spouse, parents, or children living in the US. First priority "B" candidates were kids like me – under 18 without a guardian or kids who had lost their parents and were orphaned.

Second priority, "A" candidates were adults who had relatives in the USA or another foreign country, such as a brother, mother, cousin or uncle. Priority 3 candidates were those who had been soldiers in the South Vietnamese Army. Priority 3B were the soldiers' family members. The rest of the refugees had to wait for whichever country was willing to pick them up.

Some people didn't want to go to certain countries even if they were offered resettlement there. They wanted to wait for the country where they had relatives. After 100 years of colonial rule, many refugees didn't want to face racism in France, even if they were invited to go there. Almost everyone wanted to come to the United States. Australia and Canada were popular, too. I didn't even know where these countries were. I just had my heart set on the USA because my mother told me that my older brother David was living there.

When low priority people didn't want to wait in the camp for an invitation from their preferred country, they would agree to go someplace else. Some people had been waiting for up to two years, but still didn't mind waiting for the USA. They would wait in the camp forever on the hope that the US might pick them up. These people took a chance, and a lot of them were unlucky because every week higher-priority people were arriving at the camp.

By late 1978 and 1979, the US government said that they would be taking more of the lower-priority candidates. The USA picked up kids like me the most. By 1979 up to 15,000 refugees were leaving each month. In total, between 1975 and 1995 approximately two million people fled Vietnam. About 800,000 of them arrived safely by boat in some other country and most resettled abroad. The largest recipient was the United States: over 458,000 refugees from Vietnam were eventually resettled there.

In the refugee camp, it was the openness and willingness of America that we talked about the most. We called it the "American Heart."

❖

At night it was very quiet and we could hear the noises. We knew what was going on. The director of the camp, I think he was a colonel, was in charge of all the files. He knew all the names, he knew which women were alone or with their kids or brothers; he knew which ones were without a husband.

At night, he would come into the camp. He was a dark-skinned Malaysian guy wearing a green uniform, a big guy with a moustache, probably in his early 50s. He smoked a wooden pipe, walked with a cane and always carried a 45 Magnum handgun in a holster. Everyone knew that he had a gun and they were afraid of him.

He would come in, sit down, and start talking with a family. He'd put his gun down on the table. Then he'd say he was going to "stay with" them. He would take one of the girls and force her right there. The family would go away and walk around while he was raping the girl. People were afraid of him, because so many families were stuck in the camp without interviews from countries. They didn't want their files to go to the bottom of the pile. The families, even the mothers and fathers of the girls, couldn't do anything to stop him. They were desperate to leave.

It was normally so quiet at night. But on those nights, we could hear her. "No, no, no…" We heard sounds like pushing noises. We couldn't see through the mosquito nets people put down at night, but we could sense the struggle. Afterwards, he would leave, and we would hear soft crying and sniffling.

There was a pretty girl next door to me with an older father. It was a full moon one night, and I could see the director of the camp lighting his pipe as he went into her room. She didn't make a noise.

Later, I heard her father ask her, "Why didn't you scream?" She said, "If I scream, our file will go down to the bottom of the pile. If we make him happy, we have a chance for an interview and to start our lives over."

When refugees came to the camp they would normally get interviews with country representatives within the first month and a half. But people who rejected the director's advances would never get called.

Women who screamed or didn't let the director have his way stayed in the camp for a long, long time. Their names never got on the list for an interview. If a father complained about the rape, he would find that his family file would go to the bottom of the pile. And those that didn't complain – their files went to the top. Those families left fast.

Many of the girls in the refugee camp had already been raped by pirates. After surviving that, virginity didn't matter anymore. Everything was turned upside down.

The next day in the coffee shop you would hear gossip: "Last night, the director went into tent number 9. Oh, he had fun last night." The family members would be really embarrassed. They felt helpless, but they just kept quiet, waiting, hoping, and praying to leave the camp as soon as possible.

If girls saw the colonel walking around in the afternoon, they knew he was stalking his prey – looking for new families that had young girls with them.

Some refugees worked in the office as translators or interpreters because they could speak English. He would tell them, "I'm going to go around and check the camp for safety," but in reality he was just looking for his next victim. All of this news spread quickly throughout the camp.

Many of the soldiers were doing this too, but they usually tried to hide it. Most of the time it happened to girls who had no husband or father to protect them.

Men would talk about it the next day in the coffee shops.

"How could you let them do that to your daughter?" one man asked another.

"What can I do?" he replied. "He'd kill me, and then he would still attack my daughter. We've already been here so long, I don't want our file to go to the bottom."

❖

Some people who had been in the camp for a long time didn't mind being held back, because they were making money. They had opened coffee shops and made friends with the police so that they could get supplies and equipment to stock their businesses. Chinese-speaking Malaysian soldiers helped bring in supplies and cigarettes.

We had two or three coffee shops in the camp. They were open from 6am until 11am and from 4pm to midnight, because it was so hot during the day. Every night, seven days a week, people would hang around at the coffee shops. It was part of our culture in Vietnam, where we would hang around the coffee shops every day and bullshit.

The Vietnamese refugees who still had money could afford to patronize the shops. They spent their time there reminiscing about their lives in Vietnam, sharing stories of their boat trips, drinking hot or iced Vietnamese coffee and talking about their futures and what they planned to do once they got to their host country.

The coffee shops sold things like toothbrushes, toothpaste, water buckets, and the biggest business of all – cigarettes. You could get White Horse or Benson & Hedges cigarettes. But no alcohol – beer and wine were not allowed. Sometimes the shop owners would sneak it in, but you could get arrested for drinking it outside the shop.

Some people opened a barbershop and charged two Malaysian dollars per cut (one US dollar). Other refugees who could speak English or French offered language classes for four hours a day, five days a week for two US dollars a week. They offered a discount of $20.00 for three months, but most people preferred to pay by the week since they might get an invitation from a host country and leave the camp at any time.

Anyone who could afford to go to the coffee shops or buy toothbrushes or toothpaste was rich. Some refugees who had brought their fortunes with them from Vietnam were lucky enough to still have them. Passengers and boat owners who had not suffered pirate attacks still had lots of money. They lived well in the camp.

I had no money, not even for a haircut, so my hair was down to my shoulders. I hadn't brushed my teeth since I left my mom's house several months ago.

Every day, a camp loudspeaker announced who had mail. Letters sometimes contained important documents proving that someone was a relative of someone already living in the USA. Sometimes, the letters had money in them. Red Cross workers came once a week with medicine, and they cashed the money orders for us. The Malaysian police also exchanged money, but at very low rates. Instead of giving 600 Malaysian dollars for 300 US dollars, the police and office workers would just give 450. The police were making money off the refugees and getting wealthy.

The activities in the camp were boring. It was always the same old, same old. The same people would always come by to visit and just talk and talk. Some people made hammocks and sold them, others made little toy animals out of aluminum sardine cans and sold them as souvenirs to each other.

Every afternoon the kids played soccer. I played with Mr. Le's son, Cuong. We played short games, 15-minutes long with six people on each team. Cuong and I played good defense. Growing up, I didn't have a lot of friends, so now I kept telling myself, *whenever I meet someone, I want to be a very good friend to them.* I made a lot of friends in the camp, especially the soccer players I played with every afternoon.

Of course, everyone wanted to get out of the camp as soon as possible, and it seemed like a very long time for me. Every day, I waited for my interview. Every day, I missed my home. Every day, I missed my family very much. Sometimes I wanted to cry, but I held my tears. I saved my tears for when would see my family again.

I was thinking about my future, too. What was I going to do? There was only one thing I wished for while I was in the camp: I hoped that my mom got my letter. I knew my mom. She worried a lot about me, because I was 12 and I was by myself. Of all her kids, I was the one she worried about the most.

9 CHOCOLATE AND COCA-COLA

One day, I got a big surprise. My soccer friend called me over and said, "Hey, Phu, your name is on the list for the interview." He didn't say for which country.

"Oh, forget it," I told him. "I am only waiting for the United States for an interview. I'll skip it."

"No, the USA is calling you for an interview," he said. I was so excited! I didn't know what I was going to wear for the interview, because I only had one pair of shorts and two T-shirts. I asked my friend, "Do you have some long pants or a long shirt so I can look nice for the interview?" So he lent me some clothes, but nothing is free. He knew I could get cigarettes, so I had to trade five cigarettes to borrow his shirt and pants.

When I got to the interview I found out it was Australia, not the United States. What the heck, I thought, I'll go for the interview with Australia. The interviewer had large eyes and a bushy yellow mustache. I couldn't even see his lips.

He didn't speak Vietnamese, so I asked the interpreter, "Can you just pick me up and drop me off in the US?" I thought it was like riding the bus and that I could get off where I wanted.

"No, it's very far," he said. It turned out that I was qualified to go to Australia, but I refused to go.

"If you could take me to USA, I would be happy to go with you," I told him.

"Why do you only want to go to the USA?"

"Because I like chocolate and Coca-Cola, and because my mom told me to go to the USA and look for my older brother."

Then I had an interview with Canada. I heard a lot of people say that Canada and the USA shared a border so I asked the Canadian representative, "Can I go with you and get a ride to the USA?"

He laughed and said, "No, if you come to my country, you have to stay in my country. Your brother is not in my country, so I can't find him for you." I refused the Canadian offer and told him the same thing: "I just want to go to the USA to look for my older brother. My older brother is waiting for me."

I waited for a couple months. I don't know why, but during those two months every night I had bad dreams about the Thai pirates. They were killing and raping people. There was a lot of blood in my dreams and I woke up so scared, covered with sweat. I started thinking, "If I go to the United States I will join the Navy so I can go back out there and get them."

When I woke up, I tried not to worry though, because I knew I was still alive. After everything I had gone through, I thought, "Life is so short. Why can't we be happy? Life is so scary. I almost died so many times. When I get to the US, I don't want to waste my life. I'm going to work really hard. I want to make my life better. I will try to make myself happy, and I will make a good life for others."

My name was announced over the loudspeaker. Finally, I got an interview with the USA. I was so happy and excited! Again, I borrowed my friend's clothes for the interview. He said, "You be careful. The US might think you're a troublemaker." Was my friend just joking with me? I worried because I had refused sp many countries. What if I had a bad reputation now, and the USA wouldn't take me? I was so worried that I was on the verge of tears.

When I stepped into the office for the interview, I was so nervous that it was easy to pretend to cry like a baby, right away. The interviewer was an American guy who spoke Vietnamese very well.

"Why are you crying?" he asked.

"My older brother left me," I lied, hoping to get his sympathy. "He went to the USA and dumped me. Now I am here all by myself."

"Em đừng lo lắng tôi sẽ cố gắng tìm anh trai của em cho em," the man said in Vietnamese, meaning, 'Don't worry, I'll try to find your brother for you.'

"Was your brother in the boat with you? Did he come here with you?"

"No, my brother was not with me in the same boat."

"So how do you know he went to America?"

"My mom told me he left Vietnam to go to America. She told me to go to America and look for my older brother."

He smiled at me the way adults smile at a kid. He looked through my file and saw my request to only go to the USA. He asked me about my family, the name of my mom, my sister and my older brother, so I told him.

"What will you do when you get to the USA?" he asked.

"The first thing I'm going to do when I get to the USA is eat chocolate and drink Coca-Cola."

He laughed and looked over my papers for a while. Finally he said, "Would you like it if I take you to the USA? You qualify." I jumped up and down so much that I fell down. I ran around the table and grabbed him and hugged him. And this time I really cried.

"Don't cry," he told me.

"This is a happy cry!" I said.

He told me that my name would appear on a list posted in the camp, telling me when it was time to leave. "Then a bus will come pick you up," he explained.

In the camp, a lot of people wanted to leave. They chose an alternate country if they didn't get their first choice, which was usually the USA. Second and third choices were typically Canada and Australia.

Before anyone left the camp, they were thrown a tea party. Everybody came and cheered for them and congratulated them, wishing them "Good luck for your future!" People brought tea and coffee and sometimes a dessert. What kind of dessert? They used canned peas and cooked them with sugar.

Sometimes people were generous and pulled out a pack of cigarettes. But you never smoked a cigarette by yourself – you always passed it on to share.

A lot of people brought letters addressed to their families. When you got resettled in your new country, you were supposed to buy stamps and send the letters for them, just to be nice. Someone would bring a cassette radio so we could dance, and we stayed up all night long.

At one of these going-away tea parties, Mrs. Nguyen told me she was going to Denmark within the month. I was happy for her, but I was worried; who was going to cook for me? I still had a whole month to find a new campmate before Mrs. Nguyen left.

One of my soccer friend's families liked me, and they invited me to share their tent space with them. This couple, Mr. and Mrs. Le, were very nice and I moved in with them after Ms. Nguyen left. I helped them just like I helped Mrs. Nguyen – carrying water and chopping wood for cooking. Mr. and Mrs. Le were both schoolteachers in Vietnam, so Mr. Le started to teach me the Vietnamese alphabet. For the first time, I learned that "bō" means, "beef," that each letter has a sound, and together, they make a word. That's how I started to learn to read and write Vietnamese.

In the middle of May 1978, I was called for a second interview. I went to the office and the US representative told me they had found a sponsor for me. The sponsor was Catholic Charities in Ohio, and they would find me a school and a place to live because I was under 18. I had to wait a while to get my name on the departure list, but since they had already found me a sponsor, it would not take much longer.

Meanwhile, I was very happy to stay with Mr. Le. He was a small, Vietnamese guy with a happy personality. They felt like my new family. I called Mr. Le, "Godfather" or "Daddy." Mr. Le loved kids, so he was happy to have me around. He told me his story, how he and his brother escaped from Vietnam at the same time on two separate boats.

Mr. Le was on a smaller boat that held only 28 or 29 people, and his brother was on a larger boat with maybe 80 people. When a large pirate ship approached them, all the men on both boats grabbed knives and sticks to let the pirates see that they meant to fight if they tried to board. But the pirate boat sped up and came straight at the larger boat. It struck it so hard that it sank and all the passengers and crew drowned, including Mr. Le's brother. Mr. Le's boat, which was smaller and quicker, sped off and eventually outran the pirate ship. People told stories like this all throughout the camp.

Even though I had a sponsor, I was worried that Mr. Le would leave the camp before I did and I would have to move again. But after a few weeks, in June 1978, I found my name on the list to go to the United States during the third week of October. I would be going to Kuala Lumpur for the physical exam. Everybody had to have a physical exam before they entered the United States.

And then, suddenly, I didn't want to go. I didn't want to leave the people around me. It's hard to describe the feeling. I knew I was going to miss the refugee camp, Mr. Le, his family, and all my soccer friends.

Mr. Le held a going away tea party for me. He always said, "Phu, smoking isn't good for you," but that night, he offered me cigarettes and said with a smile, "Smoke as many as you want, Phu." I felt hopeful that we would see each other again in the future.

It was a full moon, and the party went on all night long under the moonlight. A lot of people came and congratulated me, including a lot of my soccer friends. I think I was given one hundred letters to take to America. I brought all of these letters to the US with me in a plastic bag. It was all I had to bring with me, because I only had one pair of shorts, two T-shirts, and no shoes.

10 ONE PAIR OF SHORTS, TWO T-SHIRTS, NO SHOES

It was October, and I was standing in line waiting for the bus to the Kuala Lumpur camp. I was by myself, scared, and nervous because I didn't know anybody. I was thinking, "Who's going to cook for me?" because I knew I would have to stay there for one week. But I was lucky because when I got there, I found Mrs. Nguyen! She was still waiting in the Kuala Lumpur camp. We were shocked to see each other. She ended up staying there for almost half a year, because her mother was old and she got sick. They had to wait until her mother was completely healthy before they could leave. So, we shared a tent space again. But in the Kuala Lumpur camp, you didn't have to cook. The government hired people to cook for you. Breakfast was from 6am to 8am. Lunch was from 11am to 1pm, and then from 4pm to 6pm was dinner. So we just got in line for our meals. We brought a container, and they served the meal into it.

There was one guy who served the meals, and I tried to become his friend. I kept pretending he was my brother.

"Brother, why did you leave me on the boat? I've been looking for you all over," I said.

"Who are you? I don't know you," he said.

"I am Phu, your brother," I said.

"You've got to be kidding! I have no little brother or sister."

"Well, you don't have a brother or sister, so now I'm your brother." I smiled, trying to make friends with him, because he served the food, and I was always hungry.

"OK," he said, "From now on you don't have to get in line. I'll save food for you and make sure you have enough." So just like that, I got special treatment in there. I never found out his name – I just called him, "Brother."

One week later I had my physical exam. They gave me my X-ray and said I was all clear and ready to go to the United States in two days.

In the morning, the bus came and took us to the airport. Mrs. Nguyen was crying, but she said she wished me happiness. I started feeling excited, because I knew I was going to be seeing my brother very soon, even though I didn't know where he was.

I was just a country boy, and I had never been in an airport. When we got there, I met the USCC group (my sponsors) with about 40 Vietnamese guys. The leader was a US citizen born in Vietnam, so he also spoke English. I was supposed to follow the group, but I kept stopping and looking around the airport and I got lost. An airport security guard stopped me because I looked like a homeless kid, barefoot and carrying only plastic bag with my X-ray. I didn't speak English or Malaysian, and they didn't know what to do with me so they held me for about two hours.

Everyone else in my group had checked in for the flight but leader was looking for me because his responsibility was to take in 40 people and he only had 39. He finally found me in the security office and he was really mad. "You have to stay with me and the group at all times!" he yelled.

Then we boarded the plane. I had never been on a plane before and everything looked so cool. Actually, I never even seen plane before. In Vietnam, I only saw helicopters. I was running round the plane, and I couldn't sit still. The flight attendants scolded me and told me to go back to my seat, but I didn't understand what they were saying and kept running around. The flight attendants complained to the group leader and told me, "They are going to throw you out of the plane while the plane is in the air." So I sat down. I thought they were serious.

Then the flight attendant served drinks. I asked for a Coca-Cola and drank it really fast. Then I asked for another one and then another one, so now the flight attendant was getting annoyed because I kept calling her. She gave me two more so I wouldn't keep calling her, and I had so much Coca-Cola that now I needed to go to the restroom. But I was afraid to ask to go to the restroom because the flight attendant might throw me out of the plane, so I held it for a long time.

When we transferred at Hong Kong, I asked the leader, "Can you take me to the restroom?" He was talking on the payphone. All the signs were in English, and I couldn't read them. He pointed down the hallway and said, "Go to the sign that has the shorter name," thinking the restrooms would say "men" and "women." But when I got there the signs said, "ladies" and "gentlemen." I went in the one with the shorter name, but that was the wrong one! They yelled at me, and I ran back to the leader.

The leader was still talking on the phone. I opened another Coke and was careless and spilled it on him. He got mad and had to hang up the phone. He looked like he was going to hit me, but I told him he couldn't do that. He finally took me to the restroom because he had to clean the Coca-Cola off his shirt.

This time the plane was a 747, and I sat by the window. I could see the big, beautiful Hong Kong skyline outside. I would have loved to run out and explore the city. The leader could read my thoughts, and he reminded me, "They will throw you out of the plane if you don't stay in your seat!" So, OK, I stayed with him at all times.

The plane departed, and I was excited. But then my stomach felt sick because I drank too much cola. I asked the leader for food to make me feel better. He said, "Just wait and the flight attendant will serve food." So I waited and waited and there was nothing to do. I wanted to sleep, but I couldn't sleep. Then they started a movie, and I watched my first American movie, Superman.

This time the attendants were Chinese, so I could speak with them. I didn't know how to listen to the movie, so the flight attendant showed me. I enjoyed the movie even though I didn't understand English.

I saw people walking back and forth on the plane, so I got up and followed them, just to see what they were doing. People were standing in the corner waiting, so I stood with them. I was prepared if they tried to throw me out: I decided I would grab them and take them with me.

When I got to the head of the line, I saw that the people were waiting for the restroom. So I waited, too. When I went inside, I tried to smoke a cigarette. When I opened the door all the smoke floated out into the cabin. They flight attendant told me in Chinese, "You're not supposed to smoke! They're going to fine you!"

I said, "I'm sorry, I didn't know." She sprayed air freshener around. Then I started drinking Coca-Cola again.

When dinner came, the attendant spoke English to me. I spoke Chinese to her, so she said in Chinese, "Shrimp Pasta." I had never heard of this, so she said she also had Chicken Mushroom or Beef Stew with rice. I asked for beef stew with extra rice. She said no, it all came prepared. "So, could I have two?"

She said, "No, one box per person."

The beef stew came with one piece of bread and one piece of candy. I thought this was so funny – Americans eat candy with their food? So I tried the candy first. I unwrapped the gold foil and put the candy in my mouth. "What is this? It is soft and a little salty. I don't like it," I thought.

I ate everything very fast – the beef, the salad, the piece of bread – and I was still hungry. Then I looked across the aisle and I saw an American guy who had gone to the restroom. They had given him his dinner late. I saw him put the candy on the bread and spread it, and I thought he was weird. Americans are funny. I asked the flight attendant for bread and candy. I told her I was still hungry. She didn't understand, and I tried to tell her what I meant by candy. I stood up and pointed to the man. She told me it was "butter." I had never tasted butter before. Everybody laughed at me. I was very embarrassed.

She gave me two pieces of bread and two pieces of butter. One hour later, I was still hungry and I asked for more food. She gave me a cup of noodles and oh, that was nice. Another new experience for me. It was so good, I asked her for another one. She said, "You've been eating a lot." I said I was still hungry, and I liked the noodles in the cup instead of the bowl.

I saw a lot of people walking around the plane and the attendants didn't throw them off, so I thought, "I will never believe anyone again until I see something for myself."

We landed in San Francisco, and we got in line to go through immigration. The leader told me that after immigration, I was supposed to wait for someone to come pick me up. "They will take you to another flight to Ohio to meet your sponsor, and someone will be waiting for you there in Cincinnati." So I had to wait for another flight.

I went through immigration and I waited and waited, expecting someone to pick me up. I didn't understand what anyone was saying. Then I heard someone speaking Chinese, so I ran over to him and asked, "What am I doing here? Nobody is picking me up."

He said, "You are not going to Ohio. The government has found your older brother in San Francisco." I was elated. They found my brother!

"We called your brother, but he is not at home, he's at night school. So you will have to wait until he can come and pick you up." Since they couldn't contact my brother yet, they were going to put me in a hotel.

I was so happy, but I was also nervous. And hungry. I didn't know what to do. As we walked through the airport parking lot, I saw lots of ghosts walking around. I was so scared I almost started crying. They put me in a room in a Travelodge. It was freezing, and I only had my shorts, T-shirts, and no shoes. A Vietnamese man told me, "Don't worry, because you'll stay here tonight and tomorrow we'll locate your brother."

He showed me how to take a shower, so I took a really hot shower and then jumped into the bed and covered myself with the blanket. I didn't know how to turn on the heater. I looked out the window and saw all these ghosts walking around outside. There were also men with black capes and big teeth. That made me very frightened. I wanted to go home. I was panicking. "What am I doing here? The ghosts will eat me sooner or later!" I thought. I was afraid the man had locked me in the room to wait for the ghosts to come eat me. I thought about going down to the lobby and running away. "I don't want to live in America anymore!" My older brother had probably already turned into a ghost like the ones I outside.

After the sun went down and it was getting dark, someone came and knocked at the door. I turned off the light and grabbed a chair to defend myself. I looked out the window by the door and I saw a longhaired witch with big teeth and a green face. I wondered, "Am I going to be her dinner?" I knew ghosts could walk through walls. She talked to me in English. My hands and my legs were shaking. My heart was pumping and I was afraid to breathe.

"She is going to suck my blood!" I thought. So I got prepared. "I will whack her with the chair if she comes in, and then I'll run!" I decided.

After a few minutes, I didn't hear anything, and I looked outside the window and saw that she was gone. I stayed on the bed and kept the lights off, thinking, "How can I get back to Vietnam? What will happen if they don't find my older brother? What if I'm going to be a homeless person here?" I didn't want to be in my grandparent's shoes, homeless, and living under a bridge.

11 SAN FRANCISCO

Someone was knocking on the hotel door again. I peeked out of the window and saw an American man. He looked human. "Go away!" I said to him in Vietnamese.

He answered me in Vietnamese. "Phu, open the door. Don't worry, I am a friend. I'm trying to bring you food. I know you're hungry." I turned on the light and opened the door.

"Why didn't you open the door earlier for the lady?" he asked.

"No, that was a witch! A longhaired witch was here. She had big teeth, and I thought she was going to suck my blood. She tried to eat me!"

"No, no, no," the man said. He laughed so hard. "I guess you don't know that today is Halloween. The people here, they love to dress up. They dress up however they want – like ghosts or doctors or nurses. But we are all human," he explained. "Tomorrow you won't see any more ghosts."

"OK," I said, and I felt better. He brought me a ham sandwich and orange juice, and I asked him about my older brother.

"Your brother was still not home. I couldn't get in touch with him, so you'll have to stay in the hotel until the morning. I will try to get in touch with him again then."

I told him how cold it was and he turned on the heater for me, and he showed me how to adjust it. He showed me how to turn on the TV. Then when he left, I went to bed and waited for the next morning.

I woke up and it was breakfast time. I looked around the room, and I thought I was in a dream. I looked out the window and saw people passing by, but no more ghosts. I slapped my face to make sure it hadn't been a dream. Someone came and knocked on the door. I looked out the window, and I saw food, so I opened the door and someone gave me a sandwich. My first American breakfast: an egg muffin sandwich, some orange juice, one banana, and milk (I didn't know what milk was).

I had just come from a hot climate, and it was so cold outside. It was November 1979. I still had only my shorts and two T-shirts and no shoes. Pretty soon, I heard another knock on the door. I thought it would be someone bringing me another sandwich. But I opened the door, and it was my older brother, David!

"*Aco!*" I yelled (meaning, "older brother" in Hakka). David was wearing a white shirt and blue jeans.

"Is that you, Phu?" He didn't recognize me because my hair was long and I was skinny and dark from being in the Malaysian camp for months.

"Yeah, it's me!" I was so happy to see him! He grabbed me, and I came up to his shoulders now. He was so happy, tears almost came to his eyes and his eyes were red.

"Where's your luggage?" he asked me.

"There's no luggage, this is it." I was holding the chest X-ray and a plastic bag containing the letters from the refugee camp, one pair of shorts, and my extra T-shirt.

"Put your shoes on," he said.

"I don't have any." David just shook his head and we left.

My brother had already signed the release forms, so we took a SamTrans county bus back to his house from the San Francisco airport. We stepped on and the driver was a pleasant man in his 50s, wearing a blue shirt. The seats were new and clean. It was a smooth ride. I had never been on such a shiny, new bus in my life.

In Vietnam, the buses were old and smelly and the roads were bumpy. Here, everything was so different. We got on the freeway, and I had never seen a freeway before because in Vietnam, there weren't any. Here, the roads were excellent and the freeway was nice and smooth. In my country, mostly I saw bicycles. Here, there were cars everywhere. When the driver stopped and picked up passengers he was friendly and always said "Hello." When people got off the bus, they waved and said good-bye.

The bus was moving fast, and I looked out the window, feeling like a tourist. Oh, and *wow*. I started to get an idea in my mind. *It would be good to drive a bus here.* I started to dream about being a bus driver.

When we got to San Francisco, we stopped at Mission and Seventh Street and walked a block to Sixth Street to a big store. It was called Goodwill. I thought, "Wow, this is a big department store!" I was excited and running around in the store. My first pick was a pair of Levi's jeans. Then I got three or four shirts and some shoes and white socks. My brother bought them for me and I was so happy.

We walked to David's home on Stockton Street, right above the Stockton Tunnel. Everything looked new and exciting. But I was also worried. At that time, I didn't see any Asians around. How long would it take me to learn English? I was used to seeing black and white American soldiers. I saw some homeless people sitting or lying around on the ground, but I didn't know they were homeless. I thought, "Oh, that's weird. What are they doing?"

We got to David's building, and I said, "Wow! What a big house." I was looking around at all the doors and balconies. I didn't know about apartment buildings.

"We only have one room on the sixth floor," my older brother said. We walked up the stairs and he took out the key and unlocked the door. We entered a small studio apartment. How many people were living there? My brother, my sister-in-law, their newborn baby Linda (she was only one month old), my two uncles, my cousin, and her boyfriend – eight people including me. They all hugged me and were happy to see me.

At that time we had no money, so we all just squeezed in there. At night we all slept on the floor, and sometimes we had to hide from the manager, who would kick us out if she knew how many people were living there.

About a week later, my brother took me to apply for welfare. After we finished the paperwork at the Welfare Department, I enrolled in school – Benjamin Franklin Middle School at Geary and Scott.

The first day, David and I took a Muni bus to school, but I was so nervous about getting lost the next day. We went to the office and the principal told us that I would be in eighth grade.

I said, "What?" I was shocked, because I didn't even speak English. The principal told David that because I was 13 years old, I would be an eighth grader.

The next day, I went to school on my own. David gave me some coins and told me to take the #38 Geary bus. He wrote the address and phone number on an envelope. At that time, bus fare was five cents for a student.

I got to school my first day, and I felt so disoriented. I didn't know anything. They told me to go upstairs and meet the bilingual teachers. I met a tall Caucasian in his 30s who spoke really good Cantonese. Suddenly I felt my luck change.

"Welcome to Benjamin Franklin Middle School," he said. "I am Mr. Bartel." Mr. Bartel showed me around the school and took me to my classroom. My first class was Mrs. Lee's class. She was a Chinese woman who left Vietnam to come to the US in the 1960s. The class was full of all immigrants, about 22 of us. *Oh nice – all Vietnamese and Chinese immigrants like me*, I thought. I felt so comfortable. They called it "second language class."

Mrs. Lee was nice, and she asked me my name. I told her, and I said that I just got here one week ago. She gave me a book. I didn't know what it was or how to read it, because it was an English book. So I just sat there and looked at people.

"Did you learn English before, Phu?" Mrs. Lee asked me.

"Yes. 'Good morning'," I said in English.

"Good," she said. "What else?"

"Sir, you have a cigarette?"

She started laughing. "Bad boy," she said in English, but I didn't understand her.

A few days later, when the bell rang at lunchtime, I ate my lunch in the cafeteria and then went out to the courtyard. I was sitting in the courtyard watching kids play basketball, and one guy fell down. He said, "Fucking A!" so I thought that meant, "I fell down." It was already in my mind when, two weeks later, the bell rang and I was rushing to go back to the class. I slipped on a banana peel and fell down and hurt my ankle. I couldn't get up.

One of the teachers saw me sitting there and shouted, "Hey you, go back to class." I wanted to tell her I fell down, so I said, "Fucking A!" She thought I was swearing at her, so she took me to the dean's office. I didn't know how to explain anything, so the dean gave me a paper and said, "Go home." I didn't understand his words, but he kept waving his hand at me to go away. I didn't show up to Mr. Bartel's math class in the afternoon.

When I got home, I told my brother what happened. The next day, David took me back to school. He asked for an interpreter, and Mr. Bartel helped us.

Mr. Bartel asked me what happened. I said, "The school told me to stay home, that I didn't have to go to school." Mr. Bartel and I were speaking Cantonese. Then Mr. Bartel went to the office to find out why they weren't letting me in school. They said I was swearing at a teacher, and that's why they kicked me out of school.

"Why were you swearing at the teacher?" he asked me.

"No, I wasn't. I don't know what happened," I said.

When we got to the office, the principal called the teacher for a face-to-face conference. She told Mr. Bartel that I was swearing at her and that I was rude to her. Mr. Bartel turned around and looked at me.

"Did you do that?" he asked.

"No, I just told her I fell down. I said, "Fucking A.""

The principal started laughing and said, "No, don't use that word, it's a bad word." Now the teacher understood what happened, and they taught me how to say, "I fell down."'" Now I knew what to say.

Phu and his middle school teacher, Mr. Bartel.
San Francisco, 1980

12 REUNITED

After my brother David and his wife left Vietnam, they ended up in the Kula Tenga refugee camp in Malaysia. They had a safe trip without any pirate attacks or any problems.

For a few years, they had been trying to have a child. In Vietnam, they had seen doctors to help them get pregnant, but it didn't work. Then, in the refugee camp, she became pregnant, and they were really happy. They wanted the baby to be born in the USA instead of in the refugee camp, and they thanked God when their daughter Linda was born at St. Mary's Hospital in San Francisco.

My sister Nora and her fiancé had left Vietnam five months after me. Their trip was also safe – no pirate attacks, thank God – and they ended up in a refugee camp in Indonesia. She also got pregnant with her daughter Lucy there. Like my brother, she was hoping the baby would be born in the USA instead of the refugee camp. Other refugees were warning her, "Your belly is too big. They won't let you through the airport." So my sister prayed, and they let her through. Less than a month later, she had Lucy at St. Mary's Hospital.

After all of her kids had left Vietnam, my mother stayed there in our house in case one of us couldn't complete the trip and had to come back home. Every day she kept pretending she was a poor widow, working hard to support her kids who were away at school.

Every day, at four o'clock in the morning, she went down to the ferry to buy any kind of fresh fruit to resell. In the afternoon, she sold cigarettes. In Vietnam people rarely bought a whole packet of cigarettes. Instead, they would buy them one by one. Then after 6pm, my mom would put out chairs and a table on the sidewalk, dry fish and squid over charcoal and sell it to people drinking Vietnamese rice wine. She stayed open until midnight and only slept four hours a day, all of this just to make it look like she was poor. We had spent a lot of money on my father's funeral, so people believed we were broke.

If a neighbor asked about what she was doing, she told them she was working to put her kids through school in Saigon, to pay for their dorms and tuition. She couldn't tell them that her kids had escaped from Vietnam because the Communists might come and arrest her. Every day, she worked hard, making this sacrifice for her children and living a scary life all alone. But just thinking of her kids made her happy.

She lived this way until November 1979, when she received a letter from my older brother David telling her that all of us were safe and living in San Francisco. It wasn't safe to receive a letter at her house, so the letter went to one of our distant relatives in Cần-Thơ, and my mom picked up the letter from there.

Mom sold the rice paddy and looked for a way to leave Vietnam. Within a month she left in a small boat that was 15 meters long and two-and-a-half meters wide. It carried about

80 people. My mom said, "I know 90% die and only 10% live, but I'm going." She took her sister and one of our cousins with her. My aunt was reluctant to go. My mother said, "You don't want to go? I'm going. You stay here." But her little sister had always stuck with my mom ever since they were young, so she got in the boat. The owner of the boat let my mother travel on credit. The owner of the boat went to Sydney, Australia, so every month my brother sent payments to Sydney until my mom's passage was paid off.

The boat encountered strong wind and waves, and water leaked into the boat up to the knees, but they kept bailing it out and traveled directly to Malaysia in 48 hours. They arrived at the island refugee camp of Pulau Bidon, one of the largest refugee camps, where conditions were very crowded and unhygienic. It was also known as "Hell Isle."

My mom spent nearly a year in that camp and came to the USA via the Oakland Airport on Friday, February 13, 1981. We had no way to get to the airport to pick her up, so we asked Mr. Bartel, who had become such a good family friend. He was kind enough to take the day off from work and drive us all to the Oakland Airport.

Mom brought Daddy's ashes with her when she came to America. The boat owner didn't want her to do this, but she wrapped the ashes in paper and hid it while she was on the boat. Every day she prayed to his ashes, "You wanted to come with me, so now you have to help us stay safe." Their boat did stay safe, thank God – no pirate attacks, no storms, and no problems.

When she got to San Francisco immigration, she prayed again to Daddy's ashes: "I brought you all the way here, so if you don't want to go into the garbage can, then you have to help us out." No one in customs asked her about it, so we got to keep his ashes. We bought a little ceramic container and buried him in Daly City.

They let me return to school, so I went back and studied really hard. But I could not catch up. I wouldn't have learned anything if it weren't for Mr. Bartel. On weekends he came to my apartment and picked me up for tutoring. We would go out and eat Vietnamese food on Hyde & Geary, and I practiced English with him. If it weren't for him, I could never have passed the tests. Sometimes I almost hated him, though, because he embarrassed me everywhere. In the restaurant, or in front of my family, he was always correcting my pronunciation and my grammar.

I felt so ashamed, but I never forgot what he said to me: "Phu, if you want to say it, say it right. Because I am your teacher. If you say it wrong, that means I taught you wrong."

We went on like that for a few months, and then it was June and I was ready to graduate middle school and go to Galileo High.

I almost cried because I didn't want to lose Mr. Bartel. So, we still kept in touch, and sometimes we went jogging on weekend mornings at Crissy Field, near the Golden Gate Bridge. I didn't enjoy the exercise so much, but I just wanted to be with Mr. Bartel. He would buy me lunch and teach me some more English. He was like family.

I was at Galileo High School now, and during the summer I got my first job, delivering the *San Francisco Chronicle* in Chinatown. I delivered the newspaper to 100 families every morning at 4am.

During the second month of my job, I was collecting money and I got robbed on Fifth St. and Mission. One guy grabbed me while another guy held a knife. They took $125 and my watch. I was supposed to go to the *Chronicle* office that day to turn in the money, but I couldn't pay them, so I called Mr. Bartel and asked him what to do. He reported it to the police, and he loaned me the money to pay the *Chronicle*. At that time, $125 was a lot of money, almost half a month's rent. "The next time you collect the money," he said, "call me and I'll drive you to the office to turn it in."

After that, I found another job at Linda's Place Restaurant on Mission & First. It was a Thai restaurant, but Linda and I spoke Cantonese. So, in 1981, I was 14 years old and had two jobs – one in the morning and one after school. At Linda's, my job was to wash the dishes, clean up the tables and mop the floor. Linda paid me $2.00 cash per hour.

In 1983, she promoted me to the front counter because by then I could speak enough English. So, I started taking orders at the counter and I got to know one of the regular customers, Mr. Michael Williams. He was an American guy in his mid-30s who wore glasses. He was always very nice to me. At the counter they had a tip box that all the employees shared, but instead of putting his tip there, he always hid a special tip for me underneath his plate.

From then on, every time he came in, I recognized him and told him he didn't have to get in line, because he always got the Pad Thai. He'd just come in and sit down. So he was happy about that. We started to talk a little bit and we became friends. He told me that he was a substitute English teacher. Immediately I thought, *I could hang around with him and maybe learn more English.* From then on, we stayed in touch every month or two.

Once I turned 18, I went to the Post Office and registered for the US Navy so that I could go back to the ocean and help refugees. I wanted to have a chance to punish the pirates for the terrible things they had done. I figured the pirates would be no match for the US Navy. But I was never called.

After that, I got a job with a book company, distributing books to people who would sell them on commission at their workplaces. I would pick up the books at the warehouse then go from office to office to deliver them. If they had sold any books to their co-workers, I would give them a commission.

The books usually sold pretty well. My first customer was Mr. Michael Williams. He bought several copies of a book about the Olympics. By this time, our friendship was important to me, so I asked him, "May I call you 'Uncle'?" He said yes, so from then on he was "Uncle Michael." Uncle Michael was a substitute teacher at Galileo and one day I was surprised to see him come in to the class to teach ESL.

Then in 1984, Linda sold her restaurant, and I graduated from high school. During high school, my brother David was really busy with school and work, and he couldn't spend a lot of time with me. There were gangs that wanted me to join. After school, I would hang out with them, but I always thought about my mom. I knew that if anything happened to me, she would be really hurt. So I told them, "I won't join your gang, but I can be friends with you."

The next few years moved very fast. On the last day of school there was a huge gang fight. Police were looking for lots of kids who were involved, and I was afraid they were looking for me, too, because I was hanging around with the wrong people. To get away from all that trouble, I decided to go to Canada to work for my Uncle Sam. His father was the one who had raised my father. Uncle Sam had opened an Asian market in Hamilton, a small town an hour from Toronto. My job was to go with my uncle to pick up food from the wholesaler and then help him resell it. I worked there for two and a half years.

When I came back from Canada in 1987, I started selling matches and key fobs to restaurants and hairdressers for the Majestic Marketing Company. I got back in touch with Uncle Michael Williams, and we went out for lunch near Highway 13 in Oakland. Once I knew his address, almost every week I called Uncle Michael, and we were in touch again for the next two years.

But on October 17 1989, everything changed. That day, I didn't make any sales at all, which was strange. My boss paged me to come back to the office early. He told me to call it a day.

Normally, at around 4:30 to 5:30, I was on the Oakland Bay Bridge, driving home. This time, because I had finished work early, by 5:04pm I was already off the bridge and stopped at the light at the Ninth Street exit. While I was sitting at the red light, suddenly it felt like someone was shaking my car. *What the…?* Then I saw the light pole swaying and I heard loud noises, like buildings cracking and glass breaking. I thought I was hallucinating. After the shaking stopped, I saw people running and screaming on the street. I turned on the radio. "There was a large earthquake and the Bay Bridge has collapsed," said the announcer. It was a magnitude 6.9 earthquake. I was very lucky that I was not on that bridge. Maybe God or my father or Buddha didn't allow me to sell anything that day so I could come back early. I got off the bridge just before a small section of it collapsed. Otherwise, I could have died. One woman did lose her life on the bridge that day, and many more people in Oakland died or were injured when highway 880 collapsed. Many people were trapped in fires and in collapsed buildings.

The traffic got very congested, and it was impossible to drive anywhere. I started to worry about my mom, so I got out of my car and looked for a payphone. I finally found one at Larkin and O'Farrell, a few blocks away. I called my mom. She said she was OK, but she started crying as soon as she heard my voice. "Where are you? Are you OK?" She sounded scared. My family knew that I was always on the bridge at that time of day. "Come home!" she said.

It took a long time to get home, with all the traffic, and I still had to return the truck to the company. At that time I was living in two different family homes in the Richmond District in San Francisco – with my mom and my brother on 19th Avenue and California, and with my sister at 32nd Avenue and Balboa. That's Chinese style – living around.

When I got to my mom's house, the electricity was out, but everyone was safe. My brother was a rookie driver for Muni at the time, and my mom said he got stuck and could not leave the bus. "Here, take this jacket and blanket and food to your older brother. He's at the Caltrans terminal," so I made the journey back across town to see my brother at Fourth and King.

The next day my mom took me to the Waverly (Tin How) Temple in San Francisco's Chinatown to thank Buddha for saving my life a fourth time. I am now living my fifth life and feel luckier than ever.

In 1991, I became a US citizen. To become a citizen I had to pass an interview and a written test. I was so nervous about the interview because my English was still not that great. The man asked me, "What are you going to do if you become a citizen?"

I said, "I will work hard to make money so I can take care of my mom. And I also want to make good money to help refugees and immigrants coming to this country. I want to be a useful person, not an abuser." The man smiled and said, "Good."

On the written test, I had to answer three questions. The first was, "When is Independence Day?" I answered, "Every July 4th." The second question was, "What is Thanksgiving for?" I said it was for the Pilgrims giving thanks for being in America. And the third question: "What is the highest thing in the US?" And I said, "The flag." I was so thrilled to become an American citizen that I invited my whole family out to dinner at a Vietnamese restaurant. It was a huge celebration. My sister was so happy for me that she paid for everyone.

David was the first one to become an American citizen. After that it was me, my sister, and then my mom.

The Loma Prieta Earthquake, 1989

13 MUNI

After the earthquake, people tightened their wallets and didn't spend a lot of money. Sales at the Majestic Marketing Company got slower and slower until it finally went out of business. I was unemployed for about six months.

Broke, with no job, I went back to Uncle Michael. "I need a loan, just $350 to pay my car insurance premium," I said. Uncle Michael loaned me the money. After that, I didn't go to Oakland anymore, and Uncle Michael moved to San Francisco. I lost touch with him, and I didn't see him again until 2003.

From 1989 to 1992, I worked several part time jobs. One of them was at barbeque house where I helped the chef and did some light cooking, cleaning, and just about everything else.

In 1990, my brother-in-law and my uncle said that Muni was hiring and were going to take the exam. They encouraged me to join them, but I wasn't old enough yet. You have to be 25 to take the exam. They went ahead and passed the exams and got hired by Muni in 1992. My older brother David had already been a bus operator for Muni since 1987. It looked like my whole family was becoming Muni employees.

Then in 1992, I found a job working for AAA as a mail courier. I delivered the mail from their main office to their district office in a company car. I worked for AAA for nine years until 1999, and then they outsourced my job. My older brother David had already been working for Muni for 12 years. He still works for them, so he is one of their old-timers now.

"Why don't you come join Muni?" he said. But he warned me, "Here, you have to pass the exams. It's not like Vietnam, where you can just buy the license."

But I saw him working so hard and under so much pressure to be on schedule, I wasn't sure. I remembered that it was my dream to drive a bus, and I knew my driving skills were strong enough, but I was worried about the written test. I wasn't sure I could pass it.

The first DMV test was the airbrake test, which was the hardest. I had to study a lot of vocabulary that I didn't understand. The next test was to qualify for Muni, which I studied for using the DMV handbook. That test was an oral exam given by a panel of six people. They asked a lot of questions like, "What would you do if you picked up a senior and there were no open seats?" I answered, "Well, I would ask someone who could stand to give them their seat."

I passed both of those tests on the first try and got my Commercial B license. I quit the AAA job and started to get very excited about operating a Muni bus. I started the 3-month training with Muni in 1999. My driving skills were still a little weak because I had never driven heavy equipment before, and the language was totally different. My instructor was very strict and exacting. I was worried I couldn't handle it because English was my second language.

One time my instructor told me, "Make a right turn at the next corner. Phu, I want you to use the buttonhook." I was looking for the button. I thought the buttonhook was a signal. I was sitting at the light until it turned green and red and green again. He got mad and screamed at me, "Phu, you are blocking traffic. What the hell are you sitting there for?"

I kept looking and then I finally I asked him, "Excuse me, can you tell me where the buttonhook is? I can't find it."

He looked at me and started laughing and slapped his forehead. "Are you kidding me?" Even the other classmates on the bus were laughing. "No, no, no. 'Buttonhook' means you pull to the far left, then hook back to the right to go on to a narrow street. That's heavy equipment language."

Then I switched instructors and got a Chinese instructor. It was easier to communicate when I needed to ask about a word I didn't understand. My driving got better and better. My new instructor always reminded me, "Don't get angry when you're driving. When you're in service, safety is Muni's number one priority. There cannot be a mistake. Just one little mistake could kill a lot of people." I remembered every word he said and took it all to heart.

"Later when you're out there in service, you're going to hear two words from passengers – either 'thank you' or 'fuck you.' Don't get angry when you see the middle finger. Let it go and eat your lunch in peace."

After the training, I took the final written test and got 97%. I graduated!

We have seven bus divisions in San Francisco, and I started driving part-time in the Kirkland division by Fisherman's Wharf. My first job was operating the 43 Masonic line. This was the division in which most of my family worked – my older brother, my brother-in-law, my sister-in-law's brother, and me. Our family now has at least six people who work for

Muni. Everybody followed my older brother David. He was the first one to buy a house, the first one to work for MUNI.

This job has good benefits and good salary, and if you work hard you make more money. Some people say, "Go home to your country, you immigrants come here and take our jobs." I don't argue with them. It's a free country and they can say whatever they want.

In May 2000, I was promoted to full-time and switched over to the Flynn division. I was driving route #15, which went all the way across town from Fisherman's Wharf to City College.

When I went over to Flynn, I didn't know anybody and had to wait for the training supervisor to train me to operate the 60-foot bus. On my first day at Muni, veteran operator John Lewis came over and offered me coffee and kept me company. He was in the US Army for over 20 years and has been a San Francisco Muni operator for over 20 years. He made me coffee every morning, and after that I called him "Uncle John."

Uncle John was on a "standby run" because he had seniority. The longer you work for Muni, the more choices you get: your schedule, your start time, and the location where you want to work. After 20 years of seniority, operators can do standby runs, meaning that they only drive a couple runs in the morning or evening and are on call the rest of the day in case of emergencies. For example, if there is an accident in a tunnel, the standby operators are ready to drive shuttles to pick up stranded passengers.

It was a really big change in my life. I was getting good money and good benefits. SF Muni operators are guaranteed no lay-offs; as long as you don't do anything wrong, they cannot fire you. You only fire yourself if you do something wrong.

But this job is a heck of a job. People think it's easy being a San Francisco city bus driver. They think we just sit around all day and get paid for it. But the job carries a lot of responsibility and is very stressful. We have to put up with angry passengers, watch out for traffic, and try to stay on schedule.

People depend on us and we have to keep them safe. There's not enough time to eat properly or to use the restroom, and sitting behind the wheel all day makes many drivers overweight. After 20 or 30 years, many MUNI operators retire only to die prematurely from stress and illness. You may think bus drivers are rude, but if a passenger shows us just a little kindness, the next time you're late for work, running hard to catch the bus, we'll stop and wait for you. When passengers argue with us or insult us, then it's not safe or pleasant for anyone.

Muni pays you a high salary not for the driving – that part is easy. They pay you for putting up with the public. You have to deal with many different people, many different attitudes.

But I didn't have problems with anybody. I enjoyed driving and dealing with the public very much, because I love people. I worked really hard. I took good care of seniors and disabled people and made sure they had a seat before I took off.

❖

One bright Sunday in October 2000, I was working the twilight shift from afternoon until midnight. There was lots of traffic and lots of people coming home from church. I had just left Fisherman's Wharf, and I stopped to pick up an old lady with white hair. I lowered the steps for her.

"Hi, Phu," she said, as she struggled up the three steps with her cane.

"Good morning!" I said.

"It's afternoon now," she corrected me, and we both laughed.

"Mama, please sit down now," I called in a loud voice over my shoulder.

I checked the mirrors, and before I pulled out, I checked if anyone was on the right side because we often get passengers chasing the bus at the last moment. I didn't see anyone. Then I looked over my left shoulder one more time and called, "Hold on please!" An automated voice echoed the same phrase in English, Cantonese and Spanish. I pulled out and smoothly joined all the Sunday traffic.

We were headed toward SoMa. At the next stop some of my regular passengers got on: two elderly Japanese ladies, one with really short salt and pepper hair and a walker.

"Here, Phu, this is for you," she said, and she handed me a little plastic bag with a piece of chocolate cake inside.

"Oh! I love chocolate cake," I said.

"I got it for you this morning before I went to church."

"Thank you!" I smiled and put the cake with my lunch. She was always very kind and brought me treats on Sundays.

It was about 2pm and my bus was packed – standing room only. I was going downhill on Geneva Avenue, and we had already passed City College, nearing the end of the route. I could hear a bunch of kids in the back of the bus messing around. In those days, there was an emergency switch at the top of the rear door (since then, Muni has removed it). The kids pulled the emergency switch as a joke, the door opened, and the bus automatically screeched to a halt. Everybody who was standing on the bus fell down.

A man who was standing just behind me fell forward and hit his head on the fare box really hard. It must have really hurt. I turned to the guy and said, "Are you OK?" He slowly stood up, one hand rubbing the front of his head, the other hand holding a glass bottle inside a paper bag. He didn't say anything. Suddenly he whacked me on the side of my head with the bottle, and I blacked out.

When I woke up, I was in the hospital with my head swollen as big as a watermelon. I had a cut above my left ear where I got 15 stitches. The guy who whacked my head had run away. Apparently, he thought that I was a rookie and that I had intentionally jammed the brakes, causing him to fall.

I was in the hospital for two days. When I got out of the hospital, I went home to my mother's house in the Richmond District in San Francisco. She cried and cried, "Oh, my poor baby!" (I'm her youngest son). She kept checking on me all night, asking how I was, and if I needed something to eat.

After I got out of the hospital, I kept getting headaches. Every time I got a headache, I lost my vision for a couple seconds. Everything just got dark in front of my eyes. I had to go on disability, and I couldn't operate a bus anymore.

For a whole year, almost every night, I dreamed that I was back on the boat. I saw the pirates. I saw the blood, the knives, the women screaming, and the old people sobbing. While I was on the boat, I never let fear get to me. Now, I was thinking about it all the time, whether I wanted to or not. I had never had those flashbacks before, and it really disturbed me. I was waking up screaming in the middle of the night, sweating. My mom thought I was going crazy.

During that year on disability, every day I hung around at Hockey Haven. Hockey Haven is a small neighborhood bar in the Richmond District, on 38th and Balboa. It's a sports bar with five TVs, all tuned to different sports, and a little patio out back. There was a game there called Golden T Golf that cost $3.00 for 18 holes. Yeah, I had nothing else to do.

The owner, Josephine, was like a godmother to me. She adopted me in 1989 right after the earthquake. Her husband, my "godfather," is John Finley. John and Jo treated me like their son and helped me with everything, like tax forms. And when I was broke, they loaned me money. They trusted me.

Every day I went to the bar and had my regular – a "Heikodin." That's a Heineken with a Vicodin painkiller. I used to play pool with John, and we'd play for drinks. He was a lot better than me – he'd win seven out of 10 times. I knew he'd beat me, but I wanted to buy him a drink to make him happy, to say thank you.

There was a nice, pretty bartender there named Erin Massey. She could read the customers' minds and always knew what you wanted before you asked. She was always thinking of ways to make the bar more fun, so Monday night football steak nights were born. The steak was cheap and fresh, and they only sold 60 cuts so you had to get there early. A big rib eye dinner was $12. It came with a baked potato and salad and was a lot cheaper than a regular restaurant. People came early on Monday nights to get good seats for the football games, and we had fun watching them.

So this was the bar where my social life took place – and my rehabilitation. The Richmond District is where I grew up, so everybody knew each other. Even after I got better, before I bought a home in Antioch in 2009, I still spent my weekends at Hockey Haven. It felt like my second home because John and Jo were so good to me.

I met a woman named Kathy at Hockey Haven. We used to talk about our lives, and she said she helped people write books. I started talking about the pirate attacks and the boat, and she said she wanted to help me write my story. We began to write down what happened. Since then, she got sick, and we lost touch. But I will never forget her.

Talking about what happened helped, but it wasn't enough. I had to complete this book. Because at night, I still dreamed about the pirates.

14 MARRIAGE

After the assault happened in 2000, it took a year to recover. Then I was able to come back to work. I started driving the 38 Limited and the 38 Regular, a route that runs all the way east and west through the city on Geary Street and loved every minute of it. I was so excited to see my passengers and always greeted them with a smile. I didn't have a lot of friends when I was little because I couldn't go to school, so now I thought of each passenger as a new friend. After 16 years, I got a Muni commendation for having a perfect driving with no accidents and no falls onboard.

One day in 2003, a passenger said, "Wait – there's someone running to catch your bus." I opened the door, and it was Uncle Michael! Oh, my God, I was so happy. We had been out of touch since the earthquake. I got his phone number again, and we went out for lunch. He had forgotten about the $350 he loaned me in 1989. It had been 14 years already, and he was surprised when I paid it back.

In 2004, I was driving route 38 Regular late at night. Almost every night there was a passenger chasing my bus as I was pulling out, but I couldn't stop, because I had to stay on schedule. One evening I pulled in early at 42nd Avenue and turned off the light. A voice said, "Excuse me. I want to get off at 44th Avenue," and I was shocked because she was sitting right behind me. When I had looked in the center mirror, I hadn't seen anybody and that's why I turned off the light.

She was a petite Japanese woman in her 30s. I said, "Oh, I'm sorry. I didn't see you." Then I turned the bus around and dropped her right in front of the place where she lived.

She said she worked as a clerk at the St. Francis Hotel and finished work at 11pm. My schedule was to be at Powell and Geary at 11:01, so when she finished at 11, there was no way she could catch my bus.

"I've been chasing your bus almost every night!" she said.

"Oh, really, so that was you?"

"Yeah. A lot of times I tried to get out of work early to catch your bus, because if I miss it, I have to wait almost an hour for the next one. And I have nursing school early morning the next day."

"OK," I told her, "I'll wait for you and leave a little late. But if I wait for you, I'm going to be working really hard, because if I'm running late, I'll have a lot more passengers." She smiled and seemed happy.

So, every night I waited for her, and she really appreciated it. She saw that I tried really hard to help her, and we became friends. Her name was Lena. Then I asked her to go out. Our first date was a Monday night. We went to Hockey Haven and had a few drinks. Then the next day we went out for lunch at Mel's Drive-In, our first meal together. We dated for a couple years and got married in 2006.

We wanted to have a child, but Lena miscarried twice. It was very sad. So I took her to the Tu Vien Kim Son

Vietnamese Monastery in Watsonville. It reminded me of the monastery I lived in when I was a kid in Vietnam. There is a big statue of Buddha there, with an infant on his shoulder and babies happily playing on him. I rubbed the statue and pretended to grab one of the babies and place it inside Lena's belly.

Soon after that, she got pregnant. She almost lost the baby, but our daughter Aimee was born healthy in 2009. I believe the Buddha's power kept her safe and strong. I did the same thing two years later when we visited the temple again, and our daughter Mia was also born healthy in 2011.

While Lena was pregnant with Aimee, we went to Antioch to look for a house because one of my co-workers, Mel Duma, lived there. He was trying to get me to buy a house.

"Just move over to Antioch and we can carpool to work together," he said.

"But I don't know anything about buying a house," I told him. I had never owned one before.

"No problem, I'll help you out with anything you can't do." Mel took me to a real estate agent. We looked at many houses, but nothing seemed right for us. The first time we stepped inside this house on Mallard Way, Lena had a very good feeling. She felt like the baby wanted this house. At Mallard Way, Lena told me, "Honey, Aimee wants this house, because I feel her kicking me." So we bought the house.

We asked the monk at a Japanese temple in Sacramento to pick the best day for Aimee to be born. He had a book that told him the best days to have a wedding or buy a house or for a baby to be born. The monk said the best day for the baby to be born would be from July 10 to 13. So we picked the day Aimee was to be born and forced labor 10 days before the due date. She was born on July 12, 2009 at 4:30 in the morning. It was a Sunday. In Chinese culture, Aimee was born in the Year of the Cow, so normally Aimee would have to work really hard; but because she was born on a Sunday, the monk said the prediction was different and she wouldn't have to work at all. She would be a princess!

❖

After I Lena and I married, I found out she was a different person. We were from different cultures, and the Japanese have always looked down on the Chinese. She came from a rich family in Japan, and I'm from a poor Chinese family. She felt like we needed expensive things, but I don't need too much – just simple food and simple things, and I'm happy.

But, we had a big house to take care of and two children, so things were expensive. She worked part-time as a nurse, and I left at 5am and came home at 8pm, feeling really tired. We started arguing about money. We just kept arguing and arguing until we finally ended up getting a divorce in 2012.

Even though the divorce has been painful, I love my job and I have a good life. Everywhere I go, there are always good people and good friends around me to back me up. I feel lucky. Muni is my whole life now, because English is my second language, and this is the best job for an immigrant like me. I love people, and I love to meet people.

After I worked as a bus operator for a while, I found out that the senior passengers need a lot of help, and that made the job more interesting for me.

I take good care of the seniors to make sure that Buddha takes good care of my mom. She is 87 years old now, but she travels around the world by herself and is very strong. She is very independent and happy. She lives in a senior home in San

Francisco where most of the residents are Chinese. My mom teaches the other seniors how to knit or do Tai Chi, and sometimes she helps them out when they're a little short on the rent.

Thank God for taking care of my mom. If you ask my mom about those days on the boat, or when her son and other children left, and how worried she was about her son, tears come to her eyes and she can't speak. She is grateful that all of her family survived. And her husband, God rest his soul, his ashes protected her all the way.

I love my two daughters, Aimee, who will be eight in July, and Mia, who will be seven in December. They look like twins. My ex-wife has custody, because of my work schedule, which is from 7am to 7pm, but I see my girls every other week. That's a special time for me. We love to be together, and they always ask to spend extra time with me.

They're very smart. When Aimee visits me, she always goes to my Buddha statue and bows. I trained her to do this when she was two. I pay a lot of child support, but I don't mind. It's to assure that my children will have clothes and won't be hungry. And this house I live in here in Antioch belongs to my girls. If I ever marry again, my new wife will have to accept this.

❖

In 2013, I went back to Vietnam to see if anyone I knew was still alive, especially Mr. Han, the pineapple farmer who'd saved my life. I asked directions at a coffee shop, and someone guided me to Mr. Han's house. I was so happy and excited to see that he was still alive and healthy at 71 years old. I said, "Remember me? I was poisoned and you saved my life!" It had been over 30 years since he last saw me. He never knew if I had survived the journey.

"Oh, it's you!" he said and shook my hand. He had a lot of questions to ask me: Where do you live? Do you have kids? Where do you work? He had tears in his eyes. His wife was so happy to see me, too. She said, "Oh, Phu, what good luck to see you again!" I thought about giving them money to repay them for their kindness, but I saw that they were already pretty well off, and I didn't want to insult them.

Reunited with Mr. Han, the pineapple farmer who saved Phu's life when he was 12 years old. Vietnam, 2013

If I compare my life from 1979, when I first got to the United States, until now in 2017, I feel so blessed. When I first got here, I had nothing except one pair of shorts and two T-shirts, no shoes, and no English. And now I've got everything. I've got a good job, a beautiful house, two beautiful daughters, and all of my family is here. What can I complain about? Nothing. Nothing can make me sad, angry, or regretful.

All of my family is thriving. Even the next generation is successful, because my father was good – he helped a lot of people without expecting anything in return. That's why God has watched over us. My older brother David's daughter, Linda, leads a good life as a registered nurse and she married a doctor. My sister's daughter, Lucy, is a pediatrician now and her son, Richard, has a degree in computer science.

After several near-death experiences, including surviving a small boat at sea packed with hundreds of people, it turned out to be an angry passenger who nearly took away my dream. I forgive him, though, because my father taught me to be patient with all people, even when they are unkind to you.

"You never know what people might be going through," my father used to say. He also taught me that if someone does something bad to you, you are repaying a debt from a past life. So, you can't be mad at that person any more. Now you are even.

I thank my parents for all the good they did, and I thank God for taking care of us. I want to follow in my father's shoes and help anyone I can. Thanks, USA and God bless you. You gave me a new life.

ABOUT THE AUTHOR

Phu Truong was only 12 years old when he fled Vietnam alone aboard a small fishing boat overloaded with 260 passengers. He survived Thai pirate attacks and near starvation and spent months in a Malaysian refugee camp before landing in San Francisco in 1979, where he was miraculously reunited with loved ones.

From his first SamTrans bus ride from the San Francisco International airport, Phu dreamt of becoming a bus driver and helping people like his father, a respected healer in Truong's hometown. Now a veteran San Francisco Muni bus Operator of the Year with a 16-year safety commendation, Truong is one of the best-loved Muni drivers among his passengers because of his sunny disposition and friendly, helpful nature.

Of Hakka Chinese origin, Truong practices the Buddhist principles he learned from his father and from the monks he lived with as a small, sickly child: *what goes around comes around.*

GOOD MORNING, USA

TWO
WORLDS
PRESS